Finding the Gypsy in Me

Tales of an International House Sitter

by

Teresa Roberts

Creative Paths to Freedom
www.findingthegypsyinme.com

ISBN: 0615557619
EAN-13: 9780615557618

for my two girls, Lilly and Jessica

On the Walls of Vysehrad Park in the city of Prague

Table of Contents

Dear Reader,

This book is about my world travels and the international house-sitting business that helps to make these travels possible. It is also about my choice to retire early and my efforts to reinvent myself. I knew that I wanted to spend a lot of time exploring this amazing planet before I was too old to enjoy it! Once I was able to imagine what I wanted my new life to look like, I started exploring ways to make that happen. Ultimately, I discovered a most unconventional method to make my dreams come true.

I am glad that you have chosen to take a peek at my book. Maybe you will not get past this first page, but something drew you to open this little book and begin reading a passage or two. Let me venture a guess as to why. Perhaps you have longed to spend your winter months relaxing in the south of France. Maybe you have fancied the idea of living in Ireland for a while. It could be that your simpler tastes run to an occasional, inexpensive travel-experience, returning at the end of a month or even a few weeks to your own home.

Whether your fantasies are exotic in nature or of a simpler sort, I urge you to read a bit further. I have written this book for you. I am living proof that one does not have to be independently wealthy to travel and see this amazing world. Nor does one have to save for several years a huge sum of money only to blow it all in a few short weeks by falling into the tourist traps that often seem the only way to take a vacation. I am not a tourist, yet, I have traveled the world for months on end for over five years now. I plan on doing it for many years to come.

She must be well off, you are thinking right now. I understand that what I have just said sounds incredible, to say the least. Trust me when I tell you that I have not been the recipient of an inheritance nor have I managed to make oodles of money over my lifetime of work. I lived most of my adult life, while I was raising my family, in a rural part of the great state of Maine, where outstanding natural beauty is abundant, but monetary opportunity is scarce. I raised a nice family, sent them to college, built a modest home, and worked most of my life as an elementary teacher in a rural school. I retired at fifty-four after completing the last six years of my career as a principal of an elementary school. I started collecting my state pension early. Of course, I took a hit to my full pension due to the fact that I had retired about five and a half years early. I had a little money that I'd saved through the years, but I do not have large sums that would make your head spin with envy. I did recently sell my house, sheer luck in this economy, but I do not believe that owning a home would make my current way of life impossible. I just enjoy traveling so much that I prefer to have no ownership issues as I indulge this passion of mine for many years to come.

Are you intrigued yet? If you answered yes to my question then let me say that you are not alone. No matter where I am, whether on a bus, in an airport, standing in line at the grocery store, or hanging with my friends, when I am asked what I do for a living, and I answer that I am an international house sitter, the clock stops! From that point on, I know that I will be required to spend at least thirty minutes explaining to people just what it is that I do and how do I do it. Everyone is in awe. Many express an interest in doing it, too.

I am sharing my story with you and anyone else who thinks that they might be interested in an alternative life style that supports a new way of thinking about money, time, and travel. I have been so happy with my new life! If you hate to travel, this book may not be for you. If you have always yearned to see other parts of the world before you die, read a little further. I promise that you will find this book to be interesting and practical. Why leave adventuring to the rich and the famous!

In The Beginning

This is my story. Yours will read differently. Although every adventurer's story is unique, all adventures have the same liberating potential. Let me tell you mine.

About six years ago, I made a radical decision. I determined through a great deal of thought that I wanted to retire early. Yes, I took a hit to my pension. Yes, I was scared. No, I do not regret it.

Now, do not get me wrong. I liked my job as much as most people. It was needed to support my family, and I was pretty good at it, I think, but I had a dream. I wanted to travel, not just sometimes for designated holiday breaks, but a lot. If truth be told, I wanted to be away from home more than I was home. That was my fantasy. I wanted to be living in exotic locations not as a tourist but as part of a community, enjoying everyday life in a very new way. I dreamed of Italy and Malta and the Mediterranean Sea. My head was inside travel books most of the time. I knew that the gypsy in me was happiest when I was either planning a trip or on a trip.

Life is short. I knew what I wanted. So, I did some research and then got started. The starting part is the most crucial and necessary element to any plan. For some reason that I cannot name, I found the courage to start. The rest is history. If I had never started, I would have a different story to tell, but it might have a few more regrets attached to it. Be that as it may, my adventures began.

My first experiment with freedom was in 2006 when my husband and I went to Europe for a year. Oh, yes, I have a husband and trust me when I say that his income is not bigger than mine. His social security will be much less than my state pension when he is finally eligible, quite a few years down the road. I convinced him to quit his job and go to Europe with me. From the end of June until the following March, we lived in four different countries. Remember, this was in the beginning. It has taken time and considerable experimentation on our parts, but over the years our approach to life on the road has evolved into something quite extraordinary.

We started in Spain. My husband loves flamenco guitar. I love Spanish. We lived for ninety days in a little whitewashed mountain village in Andalucía. While drinking a cold beer in an outdoor café, we could see the Mediterranean Sea about twenty-five kilometers down the twisting, mountain roads. On a very clear day, we could see Morocco. Our second stop was in Ireland. We left behind the hot, dusty roses of Spain and stepped off the plane into the fresh greenness of the Irish countryside. We rented a sweet little house outside Tralee on the mouth of the Dingle Peninsula. After that, we spent almost a month in the fabulous city of Prague at Christmas time. What magic! Our last stop was the tiny island of Malta where we rented a 400-year-old house for nearly three months, again. We did all of this on my smallish income of about $2100 a month, in spite of the poor exchange rates. We also still owned a home and had a few bills back in the states. The money was tight, but that first year taught us so much.

Most of this first and very brave year was planned directly from my laptop computer. I picked places to visit based on interest, but the exact location within each country was sort of like playing pin the tail on the donkey. After researching various regions in Spain and Ireland, I started looking for a holiday house that I could afford. The little mountain village of Competa, Spain was a total mystery to us. I was able to see pictures of the village and read about it, but there were many similar little whitewashed villages. Eventually, I just had to pick one. I can honestly say that I was never disappointed in any place that I finally landed. The pictures online were usually a fair depiction of the real house or apartment, the exchange with the owners was pleasant and without problems, and each new region, upon arrival, was always what I had hoped it would be. The world of the internet is amazing. It allows common ordinary people to live vicariously. Through this marvelous invention, the big, wide, wonderful world comes into our home and sweeps us away.

Although this first year was the bravest year, it was also the year that taught us the most. From this innocent year abroad, we gathered enough personal experiences to be able to judge whether we could really consider doing it again. We had such a vast array of fantastic experiences that it left us hungry for more.

What Díd We Learn?

As I said, my husband and I learned so much during that first trip abroad. We learned things about ourselves, as well as things about the travel process. Ultimately, this nine-month experience went a long way toward defining what kind of life we wanted to live. It shaped our thinking on so many levels and altered our perspective on life, dramatically.

First and foremost, we noticed that the house that we had left behind in Maine, which was full of our collective personal possessions, was not missed all that much. Oh, occasionally we worried about the house that we had abandoned. Sometimes, we waxed nostalgic about certain sentimental memories, but the house and its contents, well, suffice it to say, were becoming less and less important. We realized that our house had assumed the stature of a large mausoleum, built and maintained to store all of our material wealth. You know, the stuff, the endless array of this and that and the other that humans collect, store, clean, and care for most of their lives. In the end, it was all an illusion. The stuff was not irreplaceable or even necessary in most cases. It was, in fact, more like a mill stone tied around our necks in our new life.

Living abroad opened our minds. We even think it stimulated our minds. Every time we relocated there was a period of adjustment that involved a fair amount of problem solving on our parts. Taken out of our routine and away from the familiar, we were forced to figure it all out for ourselves. We benefited from that process on many levels. It increased our confidence. We also like to think that it saved some gray cells from simply dying from lack of use.

We learned a heck of a lot about the travel process, too. We learned how to negotiate for reduced rates on rentals. We learned how to fly between countries in Europe for less. We learned where the restaurants were that the locals frequented. We discovered new and interesting foods. We found out about expatriate health insurance. We figured out how to travel light.

The biggest surprise of all, perhaps, was the realization that we could live quite easily without a car. Public transportation tends to be more readily available in many parts of Europe. We made good use of buses and trains, but we also adopted the European walker mode. We became dedicated walkers. When we returned to the United States, we were leaner and stronger and healthier by far.

Lastly, we learned a lot about money. We came to fully accept that, if we wanted to save money and travel light, we best not purchase a bunch of junk. Most people fall prey to the shopper syndrome even while traveling. It is an unnecessary expense and a nuisance to purchase all the gee gaws and foo foos that most tourists buy. Good food, airline tickets, the rent, and some loose change for a bus ticket are the basics. Anything more than that can be an impediment.

This whole experience opened our horizons and gave us renewed confidence in our abilities to solve problems. It made me feel younger and more vibrant. Now, after having tackled almost five years of unconventional travel, I feel like a bit of an expert on the subject. I love telling my story. I love watching people's faces of awe and admiration. It also gives me pleasure to think that I might provide a little inspiration to those who have been hesitant to take a risk of their own.

Along Came the House Sitter

Our first year abroad changed our lives. That is no overstatement either. From that point on, we knew that not only did we desire an extraordinary life, but we could have it. We set our minds on taking any and all steps necessary to live this intoxicating lifestyle again and again and again.

Step number one was easy to identify. It was time to unload our personal belongings. The house in which we had raised our family for thirty years had to go. We knew that once we sold the house and got rid of the majority of our things that we could head back out on the road without ownership issues to dog our steps. While we were getting ready to do this, I stumbled across the idea of house sitting. A little light went on in my head! Could the prospect of caring for other people's homes feasibly become another means to inexpensive long-term travel? I thought it was worth exploring.

Next, I took a rather daring step forward. I responded to my first ad for a house sitter. It was in East Sussex, England. I wrote a simple email expressing my interest, not really believing that my first and only enquiry would result in a return email. Yikes! Quickly, this was no longer simply an academic exercise. I had my first serious bite already. What to do? What to do? Was I truly committed to further exploring this little endeavor, after all?

According to Annie, my first client ever, there had been an overwhelming response to her advertisement, over sixty people in all writing to express interest. We were a pair of first-timers. She had never sought house-sitting services before. She had no idea what to expect either and was just as surprised with the number of responses received as I had been to get her reply to my email. We began to carry on a dialogue through emails, at first, each of us carefully feeling our way through the unfamiliar process. Eventually, we talked by phone. I gave her some character references to follow up on. She did the same for me. We discussed multiple logistics.

Meanwhile, I had a husband to consider. Thankfully, my husband managed to see the possible long-term benefits of this new little project of mine. We quickly reached a mutual decision that I should accept the offer from Annie.

Twice, I was in England. Twice, I took care of Annie's house. I would return in a heartbeat. I have long been an anglophile. I often say that I can be more English than the English when given the opportunity. I love English cottage gardens. I love English comedy. I love English actors. I adore quaint houses with thatched roofs. I like the idea of high tea. I love cream teas. I could make a trip out of just seeing churches, cathedrals, and castles. I like the English accents that change from region to region. I love their love of curry. I am besotted with the English countryside. I rank many English writers as some of the best in the world and some of my personal favorites. I went once to Haworth just to see where the Bronte sisters lived. I went to Fowey to see the home of Daphne Du Maurier. I could go on for some time adding to this list of things I love about England. I had been there twice before as a tourist. Returning in the capacity of untourist and house sitter was the best. It was the perfect place for me to take care of my first house!

I boarded a plane to London where Annie picked me up in her car. I had no idea at the time that this was just the beginning of a very exciting second year abroad for me. I spent a little over three weeks in the village of Newhaven, East Sussex, England which lies between Eastbourne and Brighton. My major task was to care for Charlie, a fifteen-year-old Manx cat who lived with Annie and her husband in a sweet little brick bungalow in a working fishing village. I had lovely views of the white, chalk sea cliffs from the windows of the house. My chores were carefully detailed for me by Annie who had amazing organizational skills. Charlie and I got on well since I am a serious animal lover and most animals adore me. My days were passed with a combination of long walks on the South Downs with the local chapter of the English walking club called The Ramblers, day trips to the neighboring towns, cooking my own meals, talking to Charlie, having tea with the artist and his wife who lived next door, watching the boats going in and out of the harbor, and going to sleep each night with Charlie on the end of my bed. It was wonderful!

Annie's house was a perfect place for me to start my business. It was so conveniently located. It was about an hour by train to London. I could easily pass a day there if I wanted. It was a very short distance by bus to Brighton, where I went often to do sight-seeing, shop, eat out or just dally on the Victorian-style board-walk and take in the sea air. Eastbourne, a slightly more refined town with its own seaside boardwalk and pretty hotels, was an equal distance in the opposite direction. I often went by train to Lewes, the county seat. Lewes is a very pretty English town that lays proud claims to Thomas Paine having been a resident at one point. There were other equally enchanting little villages that I could explore when I wanted an afternoon out. I was proud to be using the trains and buses, heading out on little excursions all alone. It made me feel very grown up to be having this adventure and handling everything so brilliantly.

Grocery stores were within easy walking distance of my house, too. I was able to push the grocery cart that Annie kept in her spare room with ease to the store and back with food enough for home-cooked meals. I already knew that I loved browsing in for-eign grocery stores. Many leisurely shopping sprees were spent doing just that.

I joined the walking club! I knew that being located on the edge of the South Downs would mean that there would be masses of great walking paths available. Joining the group was a real treat for me. I was in for a bit of a shocker, however, the first time I met up with about thirty people in the car park at the community center early one morning. Just about everyone in the group was sixty-five or older, quite a few in their seventies. I was surprised at how fit they all were, too. I took one look at my competitors and swore by God that if they could do it so could I. These walks were generally about ten kilometers through the English countryside, across pastures among the sheep, climbing over stiles, clearing little streams, and at a reasonable clip. Halfway through we would stop for lunch at a pub, where we would pull plastic, shopping bags over our muddy shoes and secure them at the ankles with a rubber band. This was done in order to not track mud all over the pub floors. After a nice lunch, much frivolity and good conversation, the leader of the group would round everyone up and commence with the second half of the loop. These folks walked every Tuesday, every week of the year, except for Christmas, and rarely repeated a route.

Annie also was a dream! She was thorough and well organized. She was friendly and appreciative of all of my efforts. Later, when I returned to care for her home a second time, we already felt like friends. I was happy once again to care for Charlie, who was by then seventeen years old and failing. She could go away to Italy and not worry, because she knew that I had a way with animals. Charlie would not just be looked after, he would also be given extra love and attention. Actually, Charlie gained a little weight during that time with me. He had become a very finicky eater, but would eat from my hand if I coaxed him. I had the patience to do just that, and he was a little more filled out when Annie returned. When Charlie passed away a few months later while I was in Ireland, I was the first person that Annie told. She knew that I loved Charlie and would want to know.

My first job was so successful that I actually applied for my second one while I was still in England. It was arranged before I had even returned to Maine. In the blink of an eye, my little business had taken flight. In fact, from February to the end of October, I was on the road seven months total. My continued adventures included Cape Cod, Massachusetts, as well as two houses back to back in San Miguel de Allende, Mexico, and a third in Ajijic, Mexico. My last adventure was on a 57-foot-boat in Baja California, where I enjoyed life in a marina while caring for a ten-month-old Dachshund named Rowdy. Whew! It was a whirlwind, indeed. My poor husband was so gallant to stay home and work while I was gone for so many months. But our dedication and commitment paid off, because in August we got a serious offer on our house. By the end of October, I had to hurry home just in time to sign the papers on the closing. Thirteen days later, we had moved out of our house of thirty years and into a small rented condo. Suddenly, we found ourselves poised to go back on the road together again. We had a new and improved model of travel to implement, a combination of housesits and rents. Best of all, we were free of our encumbrances stateside!

Cape Cod, Massachusetts

I returned home from my first house-sitting gig for Annie feeling so excited that I was almost overwhelmed. This little idea of taking care of homes while seeing the world looked pretty encouraging. I was not totally convinced that it could be sustained indefinitely, but I sure was curious to give it a try. At the time, I knew that my focus for travel would be outside the United States, not domestic travel. I had already seen most of the United States. I figured that if I ever wanted to do some domestic traveling again, I preferred an old-fashioned road trip. Yet, my second house was arranged, and it was to be in Cape Cod. I was living in Maine, so I knew that getting to and from Cape Cod was going to be easy. I wanted a few clients who would fall in love with me and willingly write glowing recommendations. I was beginning to see a much bigger picture. I saw a website and business cards in my future. I saw high-end houses in exotic locations and referrals made to friends.

Cape Cod is beautiful. Charlotte and Mary were awesome. In fact, the three of us took to each other right away and have stayed in touch to this day. I have been asked to return, but so far our schedules have not clicked. These two successful sisters share a beautiful, large home on a gorgeous piece of property located just minutes from the beach. They are dedicated and accomplished gardeners. The grounds around their lovely home rival many Yellow Book Gardens in England. In fact, gardening was the main reason that I was asked to work for them. They had started their seedlings and then on a whim had decided they wanted to go to the Chelsea Flower Show in England followed by a trip to Ireland. What to do with their seedlings, which they had in a small greenhouse, was the crucial question. Thus, my job definition was a bit different than my first assignment. Charlotte and Mary owned two sweet cats, but they were most concerned about their seedlings.

Luckily, I had enough gardening experience to feel confident about caring for their plants. My job was primarily to keep the plants watered and fed, turn the heater on at night, and begin rotating the plants from greenhouse to the outdoors during the warmest part of the day. They needed to be acclimated to the weather before Charlotte and Mary transplanted them to their gardens. It was a fun job! I love caring for plants.

They left me two cars to use. They had an enormous house. I had full use of their computers. They had a gorgeous grand piano. I played it whenever the mood struck me. I fed the birds. That was loads of fun! I loved watching the huge variety of birds that flocked to the feeders. I walked every day on the cranberry bog paths where I was able to also view wild swans that were nesting. I went to the beach. It was a lovely time. My ability to be alone was tested. I had no one except the occasional lawn service guys and the maid to talk to, but I stayed busy and involved and rarely felt lonely. I was productive, too, because I built my website during those three weeks in Cape Cod. It turned out much better than I had hoped. When the job was completed, I had two testimonials to place on my website. Now, when I responded to an advertisement, I could send the homeowner a link to my site. It gave them easy information about me, my previous career, my skills, testimonials and even pictures. I also designed my business cards, online. They turned out well! They were waiting for me when I got back to my house in Maine. The little business that started out as a tiny little "what if" was becoming a reality.

Mexico

When Mary and Charlotte returned, their happy smiles made it quite clear that they were pleased with what I had done for them. It made me feel good about my job. The three of us spent a lovely evening together eating dinner and swapping stories. With wine glasses in hand, we wandered the grounds admiring the gardens. It was spring! During the time that they were gone, the face of their garden had changed. I will say that those two ladies impressed me with their creativity, hard work, and commitment to life. They were equally impressed with me and still enjoy receiving updates about where my adventures have taken me in the world.

Getting back to my home was nice, too, but I didn't stay for long. I had responded to an advertisement placed by a retired couple who live in Ajijic, Mexico. Ajijic is not too far from Guadalajara. It is the home of a lot of retired Canadians and Americans. Lo and behold, Helena gave me a call. She was interested in having me take care of their home. My husband and I talked it over and decided that I should do it, but this time we wanted to tie in a vacation together prior to the job. He had two weeks of vacation coming up soon. I did some research and we decided to spend the biggest part of his vacation in San Miguel de Allende, Mexico. Originally, I thought that I would be coming home with him and then returning to Mexico later, but while we were there, I decided to extend my stay until it was time to go to Ajijic. Things evolved even further. Rather unexpectedly, I ended up getting three more houses while I was in Mexico. Two were in San Miguel and the third was a job on a 57-foot-boat in a marina in Baja California. I was booked from the beginning of July until the end of October. Wow! It appeared that it was going to be possible to stay on the road quite easily as house sitters. Now, if we could just get a buyer for our house in Maine, then we could both do this together. It was looking promising!

San Miguel, where I rented and took care of homes over a period of four months, is a dream city! It is a beautiful colonial city that has been accepted into the World Heritage Sites. I fell in love with San Miguel immediately. This city is in the central highlands in the state of Guanajuato. It has a population of roughly 75,000 people with about 25% being American and Canadian expatriates. The city is loaded with artists of all types. The amount of social activities available is staggering. Every day and night of the week something is going on. The city is quite easy to navigate by foot. There are plenty of city buses and taxis abound. Not owning a car is a no-brainer.

It was odd the way things worked out for us. We spent two very fine weeks getting to know San Miguel. At the end of my husband's vacation, I put him on a plane and sent him home to Maine. I was on my own again. I was starting to get kind of used to these solo adventures. I felt confident. I used to marvel at those young girls that I would meet who had backpacked all over Europe or joined the Peace Corp. They seemed like residents of some other planet. My structured life harkens back to the days of old when women stayed at home and kept the fire burning, while the men went out to slay the dragons. Yet, really, I was not from that era either. I was in that transition group of women who kept the home fires burning, raised the kids, cleaned the house, cooked for the family and had a career. Our husbands were not the young, enlightened men of today who were expected by their working wives to share in all domestic responsibilities. No, our husbands mowed lawns, took care of cars, occasionally babysat in a pinch, just like their fathers had done. I realized, while I was on the road by myself, that I already had all the skills necessary to take care of myself. They had been well honed throughout the years. I was not a shrinking violet and never had been. I was actually an independent woman. I was starting to enjoy myself!

I found myself on a Mexican adventure. I rented a small apartment for a month from a lovely woman named Marijo. We have the same adventurous spirit. She was retired and living full time in San Miguel, a vibrant, beautiful woman who managed to conquer the world on a shoe-string budget. Her apartment was well appointed. She had impeccable taste. It was clearly a single woman's apartment. I enjoyed my month there immensely. I became such good friends with Marijo that she asked me to take care of her home when I got back from Ajijic. She was going on a vacation to Greece. Marijo shares my enthusiasm for travel. I also placed an ad with a local online service for expats, securing a second house in San Miguel for another lovely, American couple who had recently retired to Mexico and wanted to take a trip within Mexico.

My schedule went like this. I rented from Marijo for a month. Then I went to Ajijic for another month. I took a bus from San Miguel to Guadalajara. Helena picked me up, taking me to their gorgeous house in Ajijic. I returned by bus to San Miguel and did my assignment for Marijo while she was in Greece. I then did three more weeks of house sitting for the couple who were going to tour Mexico. My last assignment was the 57-foot-boat in Baja California. I flew into Tijuana, where Peggy and Joe had arranged a taxi to take me to the marina. I sampled boat life for another three weeks. Taking a taxi back to Tijuana, I crossed the border by foot to San Diego, took a bus to the airport and flew home to Maine. Whew! It was so much fun! I was one step away from being a young, fearless, backpacking girl. I felt invincible!

A New Kind of Travel Model Emerges

I returned to the United States at the end of October. On November 3rd, we signed the papers on the sale of our house. Thirteen days later, we were completely moved out. We had lived in our house for over thirty years. It carried an amazing amount of personal and family history. Our children had been raised there. The moving process deserves to have a whole chapter of its own, but suffice it to say, it nearly broke our backs to get it done in such a short time span. We literally sold, auctioned, gave away or threw away 98% of our worldly possessions.

At the end of thirteen days, we had situated ourselves in one of the very few condo associations in our area. We rented our condo with no lease required. That provided us with the liberty to move out and move on when the time was right. We now were without ownership issues, except for a few pieces of furniture and some very personal belongings. We would sell the furniture when we decided it was time to go on the road again. Our personal belongings would eventually be shipped to my mother-in-law's garage to be stored until a much later date. This is radical, I know. Please do not think that you need to follow our example. It happened to work well for us though!

After I had allowed myself a reasonable amount of time to recover from the move, I started to get to work on the intricate plans for our next trip abroad. It quickly became clear to me that if we wanted to live outside of the United States for an extended period of time, the easiest way to make this happen would be through a series of house assignments with rentals here and there to fill in the gaps.

I began to piece together the logistics for just such a plan. I had received regular invites from Annie in England to return whenever possible. I had really enjoyed that region of England. The only fly in the ointment was that my husband could not be there with me. England seemed like a logical place to include in our next year of travel.

I had also established contact with Mr. Froelich, a gentleman who had tried more than once to get our help to maintain an island property that he owned. He was old and did not live on the property year round, so it was becoming more and more necessary for him to have people living there when he was back in the states.

Saba is a tiny island in the Dutch Antilles. I have devoted a special section in this book to the ninety days we spent caring for Mr. Froelich's house. Now that we were ready to attempt a year together via caring for homes, it seemed timely, at last, to accept the island gig as a great starting point, followed by Annie's house in England, and topped off with an arranged long-term rental in Ireland. Our plans were coming together. We had a seven-month trip organized. We were now anxious to get started.

We had high expectations at this point. Our previous experiences had given us a lot of confidence. We were not feeling too nervous about our adventures any longer. We knew that this third year was going to be fun.

We auctioned, sold, and gave away what was left of our stuff. We had saved enough furniture for our little condo in Maine. Now, it was time to relinquish our last hold on our precious stuff. This time, it was less emotional. We included in our sale of items our two cars. We were stripped to the bone now. Nothing but a few precious items left that we had determined were box-worthy enough to pack and ship to my mother-in-law's house in Indiana for storage. We were freer than we had been in years. We were two very wide eyed 58-year-old kids!

My husband quit his job again. This would be his second time leaving his job behind to strike out on the road with me. We packed our bags and left Maine for good. We were headed out for a year without any material attachments. It was a brave new world!

This Way of Life Suits Me

It is hard to believe that I am many years into this marvelous way of life! My husband and I successfully completed our second stint abroad together. It was just as much fun as the first time, except we had more money to spend and no headaches left back home to burden us. Saba was glorious! We got to share England, finally. We also returned to Ireland as planned.

Things are a bit different this year. We are now back in the United States and settled into an apartment in the town where Lilly lives. She is our new granddaughter, and has the distinction of being our first grandchild. We are in love! That has temporarily changed things a bit for us. I have the privilege of being able to design each year to suit my personal needs. For the first few years of her little life, I have chosen to curtail my travels a bit. It is not a sacrifice!

My husband and I had an agreement that whenever we were stateside for more than three months that he would look for work. He is working for the time being until we determine that going on the road again together is what we want to do.

Our apartment is huge and located on a golf course. It has loads of amenities and does not require upkeep. We purchased just enough new furniture to make it feel like home. It is very comfortable here. We have both decided to be very cautious about buying another home. We would have to think long and hard before taking that step. Right now, we are enjoying the freedom that apartment life affords. When we go on the road, we simply lock the door and leave.

I have built up a client base. It was natural to receive offers after we returned to the states. I accepted one house that I was thrilled to do. I returned to Spain to care for a gorgeous home in the country, a mere few miles outside of Competa. The journal at the end of this book was kept while caring for that house. It was an outstanding house to journal about. It is my hope that the journal will provide even more intimate and detailed insights into what my daily life is like on an assignment.

I rarely know exactly what a full year will offer to me in terms of opportunities. I am sure other adventures will come to me. The other day Charlotte and Mary asked me to take care of their house in Cape Cod while they went to China. I had to decline. The dates conflicted with an upcoming trip to San Miguel, but it always makes me feel good to know that people want me back.

I have so much to look forward to as my business continues to take me out of my routine and into new and exciting adventures. I cherish these opportunities. I do not take them for granted. People seem to enjoy hearing about my adventures abroad. I want to share a few more stories with you, stories about three of our favorite places in the world, Spain, Ireland, and Saba. Sometimes we were renters and other times we were house sitters, but, either way, we found these places to be utterly enchanting. Perhaps, you will, too!

Spaín

Ahhhhh, Espana, mi corazon siempre esta alla. I have an ongoing love affair with Spain. It is definitely in my top three places in the world to live. I have often contemplated moving permanently to Spain as an expatriate. There are many expatriates living in Spain. Although I did not find many Americans doing so, I did meet loads of people from England, Ireland, Germany, and so on. For northern Europeans, the south of Spain is kind of like Florida and Arizona is for American retirees. The weather is grand and the living is easy.

By now, I have lived in Spain many times, but it will always hold a special place in my heart. For it was in Spain that our adventures began. My landlord was a British woman who had purchased a three-story, traditional Spanish house as a way to make money. Everything was settled with her before I even left the United States. I was able to see pictures of the place, and we corresponded often, but I had never been to Spain so this was an act of faith.

Upon our arrival at the Malaga airport, we were met with an onslaught of busy activity. Spaniards are generally loud and passionate. To this day, I love arriving in Spain, because as soon as I get off the plane I am assaulted by the sounds, sights, and smells of this intensely rich and gratifying culture. We boarded a bus that took us from the airport to the bus station. We then switched buses to go to Competa. Bus fare is inexpensive in Spain, because public transportation is subsidized by the government. I like traveling by bus or train when I am in a foreign country. It is fun to sit back and let someone else do the driving. I like being free to look out the window as we pass through little villages. The route took us along the coastline until we got to Torre del Mar. Torre is a very Spanish seaside town that is about twenty-five kilometers from Competa. It is a great place to visit for the afternoon. I have often thought that living in Torre would be fun, too.

Driving up the mountainside from Torre Del Mar to Competa for the first time is quite a daunting experience. It is hard to describe it to someone who has not done it. I tried to explain it to my friend Matiana before she and her husband decided to go to Competa on my recommendation. I encouraged them to think about taking the bus rather than renting a car. Ray, her husband, finds life without a car very difficult to embrace, even on a vacation, so he insisted. Suffice it to say, they were surprised and terrified driving that twenty-five kilometers of winding, twisting road for the first time, but from a bus, it is spectacular. However, if you suffer from motion sickness, you may want to take medication first. The switchbacks can make you dizzy.

That initial climb to Competa was more than I had been able to imagine. It was gorgeously wild! As I passed through other little whitewashed villages like Sayalonga or looked across the deep valleys at Corumbella, a tiny village hanging on the side of the mountain, I felt like I was leaving the 21st century behind. My anticipation mounted! I was not disappointed with my final destination.

Competa is a darling whitewashed village that is the home to about 4200 people. It has restaurants, plazas, bars, a few hotels and bed and breakfasts, a beautiful church, several grocery stores, and plenty of activity. It is a very sociable town. It is also the home to an expat community, largely, but certainly not entirely, made up of the British. There are a couple of Americans living there as well. The town's people are friendly. The Spanish are hard working and family oriented. They seem to have taken in stride the many demands that the expatriates have made upon their little village. In fact, although perhaps many of the older Spaniards nurse fond memories of pre-expat days, in many ways these small villages were on the eventual road to becoming ghost towns before the northern-European-retiree stampede. They invested their retirement funds in updating, renovating and restoring old homes as well as building new homes. Now, the young people of the village do not necessarily have to go away to find work. They can stay to help with the construction work or provide services that are in demand. These villages have in no small way been changed, but by so doing, may have also been saved.

I couldn't have chosen a better first untourist, living-abroad, experience. Competa was a welcoming, otherworldly village. I passed ninety glorious days there, from the end of June until the latter part of September. This was the dry season and very hot. Much of the region put me in mind of southern California, actually. The greens had already turned to browns. The afternoons were hot, and the traditional Spanish custom of closing all shops and retiring to the cool of one's house for the siesta was still practiced. It made absolute sense, too. The walls of these old houses were designed to be more than a foot thick, so the interiors stay cool in the hot weather like a basement does in the summer. Our house was three stories high. The top floor was a terrace. Terraces are the thing in these little Spanish villages. They provide a way to spend time outside as most folks do not have a yard. I often joked about terrace life. There was life on the streets down below, where people scurried about taking care of business, and there was the terrace world above. Neighbors waved to each other as they hung their clothes out to dry. Women gossiped across their terrace walls. Families ate in the cool of the evening on their terraces under colorful awnings. It was a wonderful carefree world above the street world where a person could catch a good breeze if there was one to be found.

The Spanish are known for keeping late hours. Perhaps the siesta makes that possible. Although the village grew hot and quiet in the afternoon and the streets were empty of even so much as a dog, the town woke up after the sun set and was alive with laughter, eating and drinking, socializing, and music and dance until the wee hours of the morning, seven days a week. Yes, seven days a week! Among the Spaniards that I have met, the attitude that life is to be enjoyed prevails. They work to live not live to work. I quickly felt at home among them.

We had our favorite haunts. La Roca, a bar and restaurant run by a much disciplined Spaniard called Aurelio, was among our most frequented. Long into the night, crowds gathered to sit outside and enjoy live music, good wines, and great food to the heady scent of Dama La Noche. The bloom of this plant opens after dark entirely to bewitch. Under the moonlight, we were serenaded by a local group call Pasa y Vino, a three-man band that hosted a singer of great flamenco-fusion abilities and a guitar player who, like many Spaniards, played stirring passionate melodies with apparent ease.

There was an unspoken routine established in regards to night life in Competa. The English would start the evening earlier and end the evening usually at a respectable hour. The bars would appear to be dead. Most northern Europeans would have already gone home to the comfort of their beds. After midnight, however, one by one the Spaniards would begin to arrive. By two in the morning the place was hopping with a multi-generational crowd of dancers, singers, and drinkers. From small children to senior citizens and everybody in between, all were happily commingling to enjoy the music they loved. If you couldn't dance you could sing, if you couldn't sing you could play an instrument, and if you couldn't play an instrument you would provide the rhythmic clapping called "las palmas". It was well worth staying up much later than usual in order to savor these joyous occasions. The darkness was filled with camaraderie and punctuated by the resounding ole of appreciation for the singers and dancers. In my opinion, it is something not to be missed.

Many mornings, we took our coffees in an outdoor café. We were usually joined by other people who were on their way to work or perhaps even a few who were recovering from the gala event of the previous night. Spanish coffee is divine. I have tried both Italian and Spanish coffees. They are both spectacular. Often we would include a bocadillo with our coffee. A bocadillo is a crusty roll that is split open and layered with olive oil, Spanish ham, and thinly sliced tomatoes. Hamon or ham is a topic all of its own. It may be best left to the great food critics of the world. The Spanish are very proud of their ham. They offer it up lovingly to those who partake of it. It is often paper thin, but always delicious.

Evening meals often consisted of the famous tapas. Meandering from bar to bar and sampling the tapas was a fine treat. Competa boasts some very good restaurants for those who prefer a meal. However, we cooked for ourselves more often than not, as that is what I prefer to do wherever I am living. I had a small kitchen that was adequately equipped. I shopped regularly at the local markets for my weekly meals. I have always adored browsing in foreign grocery stores. I can spend hours examining the local specialties and discovering new and interesting treats.

In Andalucia, olive groves are everywhere and wine making is important. Competa is located on the wine trail. Every year, they celebrate their local wine with a festival called Noche del Vino, Night of the Wine. It is a lovely few days of festivities. The Spanish enjoy celebrating and do it up in style. We participated in this event and enjoyed ourselves to the hilt. You cannot imagine the level of performers that are brought in to entertain the locals during these festivities. We are keen admirers of flamenco music and were not disappointed with the performances in the plaza. Stirring melodies and passionate artists captured our undivided attention. The night air was filled with their plaintive songs and ferocious guitar playing.

We made so many friends during that ninety-day spree, Spanish and expatriates alike. We were welcomed with open arms and responded in kind. I am often quite puzzled with how difficult it can be to make new friends in the United States. We are not set up with plazas and parks to accommodate the gathering of friendly people. I miss that when I am home. I contend, however, that I would not have enjoyed Spanish hospitality and culture like I did if I had merely traveled in Spain as a tourist.

My husband discovered flamenco music when he was a little boy growing up in the Midwest. He was taking guitar lessons, but his father favored country and western music. One day, quite by accident, he heard Carlos Montoya on a record. From that day forward, he has admired this passionate form of music. We decided that if we were going to live in Spain for ninety days, he MUST take a few guitar lessons while we were there. He did! It was a dream come true for him to get to hear so much music by so many great guitarists while he was there. He did not come home as an accomplished flamenco guitarist, but he did have a much better understanding of the music and continues to play the guitar every day.

I have returned to Spain many times since that initial stint. Of course, I highly recommend a trip to Spain to all of my friends. Competa, however, is now like a second home to me. Because I have spent so much time there, I am acquainted with many of the village people. To me, it made perfect sense to close my book with the journal that I kept during my most recent house assignment that I did in Competa for my friend Katherine.

Saba

My husband and I have done two different years abroad together. It wasn't that we were absolutely fearless about having him quit his job in order to go on the road with me, but we had weighed the pros and cons and realized that we actually could afford to do this. It made a lot of sense for us to do it earlier rather than later. The opportunity to see some of the world together won out over the stability that a familiar job might offer.

Our first year abroad together was done before the house-sitting business had become a reality. We actually pioneered the living-abroad idea for about nine months. All along, we were thinking that it would be a one-time experience. After it was over, we would tell our friends and family about it for a while. It would eventually be added to our list of fond memories. However, living abroad was much more exciting than we had anticipated. I began to make additional life changes after we came back to the United States. I wanted more travel adventures. Naturally, I wanted my husband to be a part of it whenever we could manage it. When we returned to Maine and our home in the country, my husband was able to go back to work for the company that he had been working for prior to our going abroad. That worked out well for us, but we never left the first time thinking that he would be able to just walk back into his old job on our return. We left instead with a measure of faith that something would turn up when we needed it. Then, of course, I spent another year on the road without him.

Not twelve consecutive months, but an intermittent series of about seven months where I established to our satisfaction that there are enough houses to care for in the world to keep us busy for months on end. Most importantly, a strong element of trust in our own abilities to figure things out as we go was a necessary ingredient to all of our successes abroad.

Saba had been beckoning to us for a long time. Saba, a little island in the Dutch Antilles, was a place that we had been curious about for a while. Mr. Froelich, the owner of the estate on this tiny island in the Caribbean, had been communicating with us off and on, but the timing had never been just right. Suddenly everything came together. We were free. He needed someone to manage his house for him, so a deal was struck.

Something unusual happened about a month before we were to depart for the island. Mr. Froelich passed away unexpectedly. Suddenly, we were facing our first dilemma. Were our services still required? Who should we contact? Was our first assignment together turning out to be the wrong assignment?

Things usually do have a way of working out in the end. Saba was no exception to that natural law. Mr. Froelich had a group of very trusted friends and an accountant who were handling his estate. We were contacted by several of these people and told that Mr. Froehlich's last wishes were to have us carry on as planned, no matter what happened to him. His accountant in New York City would be our contact person.

Our agreement with Mr. Froelich had been that we would stay on the island, caring for his property and pool, while living in the main house on his estate for ninety days. All bills would be paid by his accountant. So, electricity, wifi, and cable TV would be provided. There would be a car for us to use. There would also be a monthly stipend for food, as everything on the island was imported and quite expensive. We lived on the island as agreed upon, for the full ninety days, without ever meeting Mr. Froelich, any of his friends, or his accountant. It was strange, in some ways, to find ourselves on this unusual estate with no one to actually answer to and barely anyone to consult with when we needed answers to questions. We did have the real estate agent, Marlena, who befriended us and occasionally brought a possible buyer around to look at the property. We also were soon on speaking terms with a lot of people on the island. We were glaringly the new folk living at the Pyramid House.

It turns out that everyone on the island knew Mr. Froelich. Everyone had a Mr. Froelich story to tell. The Pyramid House was well known, too. Occasionally, complete strangers would just drop by unannounced to see the gardens and the view. The house was referred to as the Pyramid House because it was actually shaped like a pyramid. This is true! The original owner as near as we could tell had built it as a possible retreat for meditation. There was a spiritual quality to the estate. Living in the clouds can be very strange. Lying in bed at night while looking at the twinkling lights of the nearest island continuously created a feeling of being on a ship at sea. This otherworldliness, accentuated by utter seclusion, allowed one's thoughts to flow into a quiet nothingness that was at once peaceful and comforting. It was believable that at one time the estate had served in the capacity of a retreat.

At any rate, the decision was made to continue with our plans to leave Maine. We had traveled together in the beginning, but that was before I became a house sitter. As the time drew nigh, we were filled with great expectations for our first assignment together. What an adventure it would turn out to be!

As a young girl, I had read the stories of Osa and Martin Johnson, a husband and wife team of adventurers who had traveled throughout Africa. My husband's boyhood dreams had been fueled by his love for Jack London's tales of adventures in the Great White North. We both fancied ourselves to be of similar spirit. Of course, the time spent in Saba hardly compares to the gritty tales of our heroes, but for two late bloomers approaching age sixty, we were game to give this opportunity our best shot.

To get to Saba, we had to fly into St. Maarten airport and then either take a small prop plane to the little Saba airport or go to the island by ferry. I opted for the ferry and lived to regret it. Yes, I lived, but I have to say that the almost four-hour ferry ride was too much for me. I had taken motion sickness pills, but I had no idea what a rough ride it would be. First of all, the ferry was not big. No cars on this ferry, but cargo and supplies and a few passengers soon filled it up. That was my first clue that I needed to hang on, because it was going to be a bumpy ride. I do not exaggerate when I say that I closed my eyes for the entire trip. Every time I took a peek to see where we were going, the ferry, much to my dismay, was either lying on one side or the other. The waves were huge. I promised myself that if I made it to the island in one piece that I would never cross by water again. Nope! Never, again!

We finally arrived in the dark and were met by a taxi to be carried away on a winding, twisting road and dropped off roadside, where a nice lady standing in the dark with a wheelbarrow met us. We loaded our things into her wheelbarrow, following her down the grassy path, across a pasture, where we could see the eyes of goats staring at us in the dark, through a gate, down another rock path, where we finally arrived at the main house. Within about thirty minutes, we fell into bed and slept as sound as two drunken sailors until the morning light woke us up. I have never had a more arduous arrival to a new location.

What awaited us was well worth the trouble, I think. For the next ninety days we lived, worked, socialized and played on this very special little island. Mr. Froelich's estate was a little off the beaten track. There was no road that gave us access to his property. We literally had to walk the path as described every time we wanted to leave the property to go to town. We really did not mind as we were in good physical shape from already being dedicated walkers. This experience only made our walking more interesting.

Saba is about five square miles total. It is shaped like a mountain. It has one road called "The Road". There are four little villages and a medical school that attracts largely American and Canadian students. There is a first-rate diving school. The water around the island is ecologically pristine. Plant life is tropical. Some of the most beautiful orchids in the world are indigenous to this island paradise. There are a few private hotels and inns, but most of the tourists that come to Saba are divers or hikers. There are trails that crisscross the island. There are giant iguanas living on the island and wild goats abound. We usually had to chase a herd of goats from our yard several times a day.

The pool on the estate was a treat, as not only did it offer blessed cooling benefits after returning from town laden with groceries, but while floating in the water, it offered a view of the islands of the Dutch Antilles. I have never had such a view from anywhere in the world. We were 1700 feet cliffside. We were literally in the clouds. The views were truly panoramic. I was never able to take a picture that successfully captured what we saw each day. It was a rare treat to watch the face of the sky and mood of the sea changing hour by hour and minute by minute throughout the day. Even at night, if there was a full moon, the sky seemed enormous. We had our own Garden of Eden. I suspect that we will never again care for such an unusual house.

Most of the island inhabitants were either of Dutch descent or were descendents of African slaves. There are about 1400 people living on the island. That number could fluctuate by the annual student population attending the medical school. The island still belongs to the Dutch. Everyone speaks both English, with a marvelous and unique accent, and Dutch. We found people to be friendly and helpful on this little island. We got to know quite a few people on a more intimate level. Some were kind enough to invite us to join them on a Friday or Saturday night for a cold beer at the local karaoke bar and restaurant. A few actually walked the path leading back to our house and paid us the compliment of a personal visit. We even got invited by some of the students to attend a Bollywood theme party. On another occasion, we joined the students for a bonfire party on the one beach on the island. Although we were many years older than most of the students, no one seemed to mind having us hanging around.

People are surprised to hear that there is only one beach on this island and that it is only there part of the year. Saba is not a beach island. It is a hiker's island and a diver's paradise. We did some hiking, of course, but the diving we left to others.

My first time to chase the goats from our yard occurred after we realized that they would never be content to just nibble the grass close to the edge of the cliff. No, they would eventually wander each day a little closer to the hibiscus or the other ornamental plants that adorned the gardens. Inevitably, the locals turned out to be right. Chase them away, they warned us. So, one day, I decided to do just that and ran out to the edge of the pool flailing my arms and yelling at them to go away. To my surprise, they all turned tail and leapt off the edge of the cliff. I was absolutely horrified. I ran to the exact spot where they had been standing before they took what appeared to be a fatal leap to their deaths 1700 feet below. Looking down over the edge, I saw them standing on tiny little ledges beneath me. They were so sure footed and agile, simply built to survive on the steep craggy sides of the island.

Our daily lives were in many ways less eventful that many of our other jobs. We had some work to do to the gardens, but not as much as you might think. Watering took some time each day, but as the dry season progressed, we needed to conserve on water. The Pyramid House's water supply was provided by two cisterns in which water was collected during the rainy season. We had to become somewhat stingy with water, as the pool required regular topping off, too, and of course, we needed water for household use. We provided roughly two hours of hands-on tasks a day and the security of having someone living on the premises. Crime was not much of a factor on the island though. It was a safe place to live, really much different than the neighboring islands. Everyone knew everyone. People simply had very little opportunity to misbehave.

Our days were filled with taking care of the property, going into town to get our groceries, driving "The Road" while gasping at each breathtaking vista, or swimming au natural in the pool, as the mood struck us. We often treated ourselves to a great meal out several times a week. We also were entertained by television or pod casts in the evening. Every evening we strolled outside to sit on the pool patio and watch the sun set. That was the best show of all. Sometimes it was almost too beautiful to endure. For two nature lovers, this was the perfect form of entertainment.

There were two wonderful cats living on the property, Setai and Cleo. Setai was a very special cat. I soon became so attached to him, and he to me, that when it came time to leave the island, it was even harder to do than I had expected. I hated to say goodbye to him. He was the older of the two cats and right away I recognized an old soul in his solemn stare. He was extremely intelligent. When we returned from a morning in town, the two cats always came running to greet us. We fed and cared for them. We gave them love and attention. To this day, I miss Setai. That may sound utterly ridiculous, but I have always had the capacity to bond with animals from the time that I was a little girl. I tend to like all animals. Yet, as with people, there are those special animals who stand out in my mind as having some unique quality that I can quickly recognize, but cannot easily name. It is a kind of chemistry that just clicks. You know it when it happens.

There were lots of little lizards that played amongst the vines and plants and ran across our patios. We even had one that lived in our house. He never bothered anyone, so we allowed him to live alongside us. The baby iguanas were a perfect bright, lime green. They had big round eyes. I thought they were extremely cute. They did not grow up to be cute. No! They could be huge, some reaching five feet, and ugly. They are not aggressive, I am told, but my, oh, my how scary they did look. I suspect, when cornered, they could whip you with their tails quite effectively. However, they were basically shy creatures and ran if you got too close to them.

We spent one week with such low clouds that we were enshrouded. It was almost spooky. Everything looked magically different during that week. We passed a good bit of our time either in town or in the house. It was damp outside. Generally speaking, the sky was blue with huge cloud formations that came and went. Roving thunder storms danced across the horizon, while we watched from our patio drenched in sunlight. Swift clouds periodically rushed over us and then were gone, followed by more brilliant sunshine. Always, the islands stretched out before us. It felt just like a private showing. Nature's best performance, far surpassing anything that man could do!

All good things must come to an end, I am told. Our days in Saba passed before we knew it. The time came to say a final goodbye. We did our last round of watering the gardens, filled and cleaned the pool and patios, tidied the house one more time, said our goodbyes to the cats and climbed into a taxi to head to the airport. Yep! I kept my word. No ferry ride back to St. Maarten for this girl. I would fly instead. So, taking off in a small prop plane from the shortest landing strip in the world, we headed out into the wild blue yonder. Our next assignment was waiting for us. Soon we would be walking on the South Downs of England once again!

Ireland

We have lived in Ireland twice, thus far, and I can safely say that I would return to Ireland in a heartbeat. Ireland also takes a place on my list of favorite countries. I could easily imagine myself living there as an expatriate. It lays claims to being one of the most beautiful landscapes in the world. The countless shades of green are a reality. The freshness of the air, the utter charm of the Irish people, the wholesome food, the welcoming pubs, and the wonderful Irish traditional music are just a few things that make Ireland a great place to live.

The first time we were in Ireland, we rented a house just outside the town of Tralee. Tralee sits on the mouth of the Dingle Peninsula. There are three astonishingly beautiful peninsulas in the west of Ireland. I have had the joy of exploring all of them. They are the Dingle Peninsula, the Ring of Kerry, and the Beara Peninsula. Each presents amazing vistas, breathtaking landscapes, lonely passes, free-ranging sheep, and such heartbreaking natural beauty that it becomes a spiritual experience to encounter it.

Oddly, I feel at home among the Irish in much the same way that I feel at home with the Spanish. To me, the two cultures have some very noticeable similarities. First, the people are hard working and outgoing. There is boldness about the way they attack life. Both countries have endured bone-crushing poverty in the past. Both countries have a long history with the Catholic Church. Both countries cherish their traditional music, old, treasured songs consisting of plaintive melodies and lyrics that tell wonderful stories. Just like the Spanish, the Irish are also unabashedly passionate.

Pub life in Ireland is equally up to the task. Pubs are welcoming places. They are often small and intimate where great "pub grub" can be bought for a relatively small price, enhanced by the taste of a Guinness. I love "pub grub" which most frequently consists of the roast of the day, lamb, beef or pork, accompanied by cabbage, potatoes, carrots, and Irish soda bread. It is hearty and wholesome.

I negotiated for our house ahead of time with our landlady, Myra, by once again following my established procedure and choosing the holiday house online. For about 700 euros a month I enjoyed an absolutely beautiful house consisting of living room, fully fitted kitchen, two bedrooms and two bathrooms. It was such a charming house of almost storybook proportions and well appointed. We even had a lovely fireplace where we happily burned peat most evenings. We were there for almost three months during the fall. The evenings could be chilly.

Actually, our love affair with walking blossomed when we were in Ireland, largely due to a mistake that Myra made. I do not think it was an intentional mistake on her part when she wrote and told me that her house was a quick ten minute walk from the nearest bus stop. I actually think that when I wrote to her enquiring as to whether her house was within easy walking distance of a bus stop that she probably never suspected that we would only rent a car six days out of the two and a half months that we were living in Ireland, but that was most certainly the case. Our time in Myra's house tested our commitment to living without a car. I think the Irish are more car-dependent than most Europeans. However, as it turned out, the house we rented from Myra was sort of in the country. To get to the nearest bus stop, we had to walk over a mile, often in inclement weather, to pick up a small bus that serviced Blennerville and Tralee. Myra's house was technically located in the tiny village of Blennerville. We needed to go to Tralee for shopping, libraries, Internet and entertainment, which we did at least every other day unless gales had set in for the day prohibiting us from making that walk to the bus stop. Gales were prevalent. Strong winds and rain are called gales in Ireland. In fact, it rained almost every day, but most days that was not a problem because the rains came and went with the sun breaking out in between. I suspect that is where "the pot of gold at the end of the rainbow" story came from, since rainbows were such common occurrences. We hardly went a day without a rainbow. Sometimes, more than one rainbow in a day's time would appear. Sometimes, double rainbows would appear. Once, there was a rainbow of spectacular proportions that lasted for over thirty minutes. There is magic in Ireland, no doubt about it!

So, with umbrellas and backpacks always in tow, we learned that we were able to walk many miles every day just to take care of daily business. We were startled at how good we were at it and how much we actually enjoyed it. Needless to say, we lost weight and built up stamina and endurance, returning home leaner and more confident than before we had left.

I have never taken care of a house in Ireland, but I often see them advertised on websites. The timing and location has not been quite right, so far, but I hope to do one eventually, as I figure that I will be returning to Ireland for the rest of my life in one fashion or another.

My second stay in Ireland followed my second assignment for Annie in England. I was living so close to Ireland, while taking care of Charlie, it seemed a shame not to squeeze in another visit. I made arrangements to rent an apartment in Killarney. This time, we did loads of walking, too, but not necessarily as a requirement to take care of daily business. Our apartment was located right in the center of town, a few blocks from grocery stores and also the entrance to the Killarney National Park. What a joy! If you are a serious nature lover, Killarney National Park is not to be missed. It has miles and miles of walking paths and plenty of wild life, plus gorgeous vistas. We often would walk to the park and choose a new path to explore for the day. It was a gift!

Killarney is probably the most visited town in Ireland, other than Dublin. Killarney is not nearly as big as Dublin, though, and easily managed by foot. It is a colorful town with loads of pubs, restaurants, and bars. Most of the pubs and bars in town offered live traditional music every night of the week. We lived in the town center. We were able to stroll about after dark, choosing a different place to enjoy a beer and some great music any time we felt like going out. All that readily available entertainment was an extra bonus. We took advantage of it. One of our favorite places was Danny Mann's, a bar and restaurant, largely because there was a three-man group called Natural Gas that played there fairly often. We simply adored their music. They had a fiddler who was smoking hot. Their lead singer had a powerful voice. As is common to the Irish, they had an uncanny ability to mix Irish humor with poignant melodies in such a way that entertained the audience magnificently. It was very common to have the audience join the band and sing the chorus of some popular old song. The Irish are not embarrassed to sing in public.

Our apartment was gorgeous. It was a fairly large modern building with a nice lobby. The units were generally rented for weekends or holidays of a week or two. We were unusual, I think, as we rented our apartment for two months at the very good rate of 700 euros a month, all inclusive. These apartments were very modern, with gorgeous bathrooms, washers, dish washers, clothes dryers, and marble floors. They were spotlessly clean and quiet. We would definitely stay there again in the future.

We also met several other people who were staying in the apartment complex. We met a lone American man, Steve, who joined us frequently for an evening of beer and entertainment. We also met a lovely couple from England who were having a small holiday together and seemed happy to make our acquaintance. I am not shy. If I think that someone I meet may be interesting, I generally take the first step to invite them to join us for a drink or a meal at a local restaurant or bar. This willingness on my part to offer a friendly handshake to a stranger has paid off, because I have been lucky to meet some great people from all over the world. Some have gone on to be good friends. Others I may have only passed an hour or two with, but all have made my travels a bit more interesting.

I must mention one last thing about our Irish experience. At various times throughout this book I have noted that opportunities have come my way that were unexpected because of my house-sitting business. One of those unexpected opportunities presented itself while we were in Killarney. A touring company called Corcoran Tours engaged in a conversation with me about the possibility of our arranging tours to Ireland when we got back to the states. It was an intriguing idea, and we have remained in contact with Corcoran Tours since we have returned. It is something that we might actually try to do some day. Whether we decide to arrange tours or not, it is exciting to see doors opened to us just because we happen to be in the right place at the right time.

Reshaping Each Year to Suit My Needs

It is not often that a person can design each year of their working life to suit their changing personal needs. Most often, we have to find a way to arrange our personal life around that all important job that provides us with a livelihood. The retiree suddenly has different options. They have more power automatically to get up each day and do whatever gives them pleasure. What a gorgeous concept! I know many retired people who have full and exciting lives these days. The baby boomers have deliberately redefined every phase of life, and are most certainly doing so again with retirement. There are many fantastic and creative models of modern-day retirement available to us for inspiration. We are no longer retiring like our parents did by quitting our jobs rather reluctantly and sitting down to grow old rapidly. No, many of us are seeking to gain free time earlier than usual, but end up using that time to explore other facets of our personalities that had remained somewhat on the shelf until that precious commodity of time was finally ours in abundance. Folks are learning to paint, speak a foreign language, start a new business, sail, garden, and in my case travel, travel, travel. It is an exciting time after all.

Even working people have an opportunity to redefine their lives. This philosophy of life does not have to be left to retirees or empty nesters. Anyone can learn to practice common sense principles by living within their means and preparing for a life down the road of eventual freedom. Until that time arrives, however, planning vacations around house-sitting possibilities can be part of the solution.

What I dearly love about my business of international house sitting is that each year that spreads out before me can easily be arranged to suit whatever personal needs I have at the time. Let's face it, no two years of our lives are ever exactly the same. It took me a while to fully understand that the rules of regular existence no longer truly apply to me. I can pretty much do as I please. If I suddenly decide to stop something I am doing and change direction completely, I am free to do so. No rules! No rules? Yep, that's right, no rules.

I have completed five years of travel, and am well into my sixth year. None of these years have been exactly like the one that preceded it. Whereas in the beginning, I wanted very much to live abroad for the bulk of the year, and happily did so, this year, as I have already revealed, something new in my life has temporarily kept me a bit closer to home. Of course, I am talking again about my granddaughter. She is my first and possibly my only grandchild. She was a wonderful surprise. She must be a real charmer to keep her Omi from leaving home. In time, she will come to know that she has a grandmother that is perhaps a bit different than the other grandmothers of her mates at school. Her grandmother is, after all, a gypsy.

Who knows where I will be next year. This year I have cared for a house in Spain. It was my fourth trip to Spain and far from my last. I kept a journal while I was there. That journal became the last chapter of this book, an account of daily life on an actual house sit, a little peek into my quiet life on the road.

In another year, I could decide to head back out on the road again for ninety days or longer. I can do it whenever I want for as long as I want. When I am stateside, I have a lovely apartment that keeps my few personal belongings in one place and provides me with a great home. When I feel the urge to go again, I just close up the apartment and go. No great responsibilities for me to worry about when I am gone. No need for the house sitter to have a house sitter. I can housesit or rent or do a mixture of both. I can return to old favorite places or strike out to see new places that remain on my list of countries to see before I die. My life is all about freedom and adventure! I sure am having fun!

Other Models

I have had a ball. Who wouldn't enjoy quitting their job and traveling to exotic locations? As I have said before, some people think I have secretly won the lottery. That would be a treat, but the lottery has not financed my life of luxury. Still, the unconventional life I lead is not for the faint of heart. It is one thing to admire someone's efforts to cast off conventionality and strike out with a small carry-on suitcase to the wild, blue yonder and another thing altogether to do it. Many people, in the end, will not have the desire to lead such a life.

The most important thing to remember is that there are as many ways to design your life as there are people to imagine them. The knowledge that you actually have the power to design your own adventures is the key. I have enjoyed different types of years on the road. Each one varied significantly from the one before, because my needs and circumstances had changed each time.

Becoming a caretaker is another option. I have never been interested in being a caretaker. It is like having a traditional job. It can offer rewarding pay and amenities though. Some caretakers may even be asked to travel between houses belonging to their employer. These houses could easily be domestic or international locations. The commitment involved is extensive as the employer depends on their caretaker year round, but many amenities are often attached to the extra responsibilities. Luxurious houses, pools, all-expense paid vacations, and even health benefits are sometimes included. For a person who is not ready to retire yet, being a caretaker could be a great option.

House swapping is another way of vacationing cheaply. My assignment for the American couple who had retired to Ajijic, Mexico, near Guadalajara was also an introduction to the concept of house exchanges. They had a beautiful home and had enjoyed exchanging their home with other couples who also had beautiful homes in lovely locations. It was a win-win situation for both couples. Usually this method is used short-term as a form of vacationing in luxury.

Twice while I was caring for a house abroad, I met people who asked me to consider living in and overseeing a small bed and breakfast. Both offers came about because the owners had met me and were impressed with my story of success as a house sitter. If I had been looking to work again, the offers would have been timely. Whenever I pass out my business cards, I generate lots of interest. Several interesting opportunities have resulted. Expect your experiences to open other doors.

There are, no doubt, people who have accepted house-sitting jobs all over the United States and not ventured abroad at all. There are always loads of Americans looking for house sitters. That could be a great option for someone who would love to see a lot more of the United States. There is so much to see and do in the United States. I have been fortunate to have traveled all over the U.S. and am familiar with all but four states. Do not rule out house-sitting opportunities in the fifty states.

Never underestimate the luxury of taking a simple vacation via a house assignment. I applied for a job in Florida once. I wanted to see my sister who lived in a nearby town, but did not want to stay in her small home. It was a great option. I would have had a nice home with a pool in close proximity to the ocean. I could have skipped the expense of hotels and such while getting to spend time with my sister. I was offered the gig, but in the end decided not to take it.

Find what works for you. Just remember as your circumstances change, so can your personal approach to traveling. Be creative. Have fun!

Relax! You Do Not Have To Do It My Way

I realize that my way of leading an extraordinary life on an ordinary income may not be exactly what you picture for yourself. That is not a problem! I told you my story because I hoped to be able to demonstrate just how much is possible on a small income. Remember, I am not writing this book for wealthy people. If you are wealthy, you can do anything you please, as long as you are healthy. I am writing this book for people like myself who dream of adventures, regardless of the lack of large sums of money to spend. I hope that my practical solutions will also inspire you to create your own exciting lifestyle.

As you continue reading my book, please know that I give you permission to use any of my suggestions that you deem to be useful to your own plan of action. There are many possible variations on this theme. Find what works for you and you will be happy.

In the pages to come, I will answer some of the most common questions that I have been asked along the way about being an international house sitter. Remember that I told you that whenever anyone asks me what I do for a living, and I answer by simply saying that I am an international house sitter, I can count on the clock stopping. I also can be quite certain that once they get past the disbelief of hearing those words, international house sitter, that I will be asked lots of questions. My life seems to inspire all kinds of people.

So let's get down to the nitty gritty of this wildly exciting way that I have chosen to live my life. I have talked about what I have been doing for the past several years of my life. Let's now start talking about the how of the matter. How can you do this, too!

Living in a Bubble

I have often tried to explain what it is like for me to live outside my own country for such lengths of time. I know that other people are often drawn to the idea as well. What is my motivation to live in this manner? How does it make me feel when I am doing it? Am I ever afraid or lonely? Do I miss friends and family? Do I miss my home and things? What is it really like for me?

If I am to be honest, this way of living requires some intestinal fortitude. There is a learning curve that I experience every time I land in a new country. It lasts for several weeks and stretches my little grey cells considerably. I have to learn to find my way around a new town. I sometimes encounter a language barrier. It takes time to browse the grocery stores and figure out the packaging and the new and unusual foods. The exchange of my dollar to a foreign currency, coupled with the cost of living, takes some getting used to as well. The exchange rate is not always in my favor, but sometimes the cost of living is low enough that it offsets that fact. I have to learn the transportation system. I look for the restaurants and pubs that the locals enjoy. I know they will often be cheaper than the places that tourists frequent. If a learning curve makes you anxious, then my lifestyle may not be suitable for you.

When I am gone from home for months at a time, I enter a different level of consciousness. While in that zone, it feels like a bubble has formed around me. The concerns of my everyday life back in the states fade away and lose their sense of urgency, almost to the point of nonexistence. It is strange, but I cease to think about ordinary things like bills, money, the economy, politics, and dire predictions for world-shaking events…….all those things that tend to fill a mind with nagging worries. It just doesn't seem real. I am living in my little bubble. My bills are mostly being paid for me. I do not listen to news all that much. People around me do not presume to tell me what is going on back home. They are living their lives in their own country consumed with their own domestic worries. Their worries have no true significance for me. I am a mere visitor. I am spared! When I experience this state of mind there is something inside me that recognizes that this way of living is quite healthy for me and that when I go home I should try to emulate it as much as possible, if for no other reason than reaping the peaceful benefits it affords.

Another aspect of living abroad that I find enticing is the anonymity it offers. I like it! I like going to an area where people know very little about me, have no expectations of me, few preconceived notions about me, and usually accept me at face value. I am always interested in their way of life and because most people love to talk about themselves, it works well. I listen and learn so much. My accomplishments back home, my status or lack thereof, my personal issues do not usually enter into the picture. I am merely the nice American woman who is living among them for a while and seems to enjoy the experience. Most people are proud of their own country. They take great pleasure in showing it off to others.

When I run across expatriates living abroad or travelers passing through the region, we often have a sense of instant camaraderie. We may be different in most ways except for the fact that we share a common adventure. We are both outside our own countries. It is the recipe for instant friendship. Many is the time that I have shared a beer, a train ride, a ferry ride, even a meal while swapping stories with these fellow adventurers.

Finally, I enjoy variety. I love experiencing all the interesting things that almost any culture that is different from mine has to offer. To explore a region thoroughly and intimately is a treat. This is my life. It answers the gypsy in my heart. It takes me out of myself and into not only a different geographical place, but also a different level of consciousness. It expands my soul and opens my mind. It gives me far more satisfaction that any material things that I could desire. It is what I do with my time on this planet!

Where to Go

Like anything in life, the best way to get exactly what you want is to know exactly what you want. I suggest you actually try to picture yourself somewhere exotic with a warm tropical breeze blowing through your hair and sand between your toes. I know that sounds cliché, but try to conjure up a mental picture of just how you see yourself in your new life. Before you even start looking for your first house assignment, try to articulate your dream. Better yet, put it in writing! Then close your eyes and picture it like a little movie in your head. If we do not know what we want our life to look like, we cannot as easily find the way to reach that dream. If a warm tropical beach is not your thing, perhaps, you might prefer a bustling, cosmopolitan city with public transportation, museums and libraries at your fingertips. I can't define your dream for you. That is your responsibility.

I was able to picture myself living my dream. I was also able to talk about it quite easily. For me, my location must be a place of outstanding natural beauty. Not just the house itself, but also the region where I have chosen to spend a month or more of my precious time. I require a place where I can engage in my number one form of relaxation and exercise.....walking. I walk for many reasons. I walk to clear my head. I walk in order to meditate. I walk to get fresh air. I walk so that I can EAT. I love food. So the more that I walk, the more I can eat. I walk a lot, every day, and in all kinds of weather.

I also knew that although on rare occasions I might enjoy a shorter stint in a big city, I preferred smaller towns. I require easy access to public transportation so that I can take day trips to other nearby attractions. I never travel far when I am taking care of a house. I prefer relaxing in a community and getting to know the intimate details of a particular tiny region. Of course, I avoid, at all costs, resorting to the tourist mode. I never consider myself to be a tourist. If I want to see another region, I go there to live for a while. I can take all the time in the world to enjoy where I am at any given time. This is not a vacation which will end in a week. I do not embrace the idea of seeing fifteen countries in ten days as is often the case with packaged trips. I prefer to dally along the way, cook my own meals, walk and observe, and eventually even collect a few new friends.

I am not telling you all of this to influence in any way how your personal dream should look. I am merely giving you an example of how detailed your expectations can be long before you even apply for your first job.

Make a list of your preferences. Include things like climate, size of town, and local amenities. Do you want to travel abroad? If so, which countries and why have you selected those countries? Does a language barrier concern you? Think about the altitude of specific places and the humidity level. Do you require local bus service, trains or subways? Are you willing to rent a car? Do you mind traveling during off season? Are you able to picture yourself surrounded by different languages?

What kind of a house will make you feel happy? Even a couple of weeks can seem like a long time if you are uncomfortable in your surroundings. I always ask for pictures of the house, inside and out. I would not be interested in a place that was untidy or lacked special touches. For me, it does not always have to be a mansion. Even a little brick bungalow in a small English fishing village can be charming when the owners have an adorable cottage garden where you can take your tea in the morning.

Lastly, always be clear in your own mind about the kinds of tasks you are willing to perform. I usually contract for two hours of hands-on duties each day. I will consider doing more, but that would have to be negotiated. I will get into the whole negotiation process later on in the book. If you cannot imagine yourself doing daily tasks or if you think you lack the self discipline to apply attention to details then house sitting may not be for you. So, please, take the time to picture yourself in the perfect environment, doing the things that you excel at doing and having a wonderful time!

No Pay

Frequently, when I have been asked to explain how I have managed to travel the world, living abroad in relative luxury, without having won the lottery first, I may also have to explain that, generally, I do not get paid for my services. Shock! Perhaps people get the concept of being a house sitter confused with being a caretaker. Although I consider myself a business woman, indeed, a very productive and happy business woman, I do not attach importance to making money to my business endeavors.

Here's the deal. I have an independent income. It isn't grand, but it is enough of a retirement pension that whether I live abroad or back in the United States, I can afford to pay my living expenses. Surprisingly, it is cheaper to live abroad than at home in the United States. Because I am retired, I have time, loads of time, but, of course, no longer the kind of money I used to be pulling in when I was part of the traditional work force. This is an age old dilemma of the ordinary working person. We either have time but no money or money but no time. It becomes an endless battle for many as they try to find a balance in their lives between the two scenarios. Most will not be able to strike the balance easily. It can be frustrating. For example, when I was teaching, I had my summers mostly free, but that was also peak travel season. I was rarely able to purchase an inexpensive vacation.

Retirement brings with it much free time. Free time is a gift. There has been a happiness study done in which men over sixty-five years of age were found to be some of the happiest people alive. I wonder why?

For me, retirement came earlier than most. I had a history already of travel. The gypsy blood was inherited from my father. He wandered the planet, while I was growing up, with his entire family of wife and six kids in tow. I was born on the road. I have always felt at home there. As an adult, I continued to travel whenever possible and wherever possible. Now, as a retired woman, I have happily turned traveling into my business. I intend to continue experiencing the world for as long as I can manage to stand upright, walk, talk and think clearly.

My house-sitting business was developed with the same attention to detail as any business. I had many of the same goals and concerns, too. For instance, I safe guard my reputation. I know that it is the most important asset I have to offer any client. I gather recommendations and references. I negotiate. I strive to please my clients and meet their individual needs. I deliver on my promises. I respect a client's privacy. I do not, however, charge money.

I soon realized that unless I wanted to extend my services to only one client, and by so doing become their employee, that I was much better off to exchange services for goods instead of using the services for money model. I had already worked for employers, almost three decades of employers actually. It was fine at the time, but I was, for the most part, not interested in traditional work these days. I was finally free to be creative and find an unconventional path to my dreams.

Guess what? Money not spent is money left in my pocket! That's right! If I do not have a long list of bills to pay each month or debts hanging over my head, I suddenly require less income. My personal concept of economics has always been a simple one. I just keep subtracting until I get to zero. So, take a moment and consider not having to pay an electric bill, rent or house payment, Internet connection, telephone, water bill, or trash bill. Now take that a step further. Consider not having to buy car insurance or even putting gas in a car for months at a time. What about already having your larder stocked for you? How about no cable TV or satellite dish bills? See what I mean? When all of those things are removed from your "have to pay" at the end of month list, you have a lot of money left in your pocket. It is incredible!

I eventually took this idea probably about as far as a person could go with it. I sold my home and 98% of what I had acquired in life and hit the road without any ownership issues at all. That third year was like being seventeen again, but with money. I had no ties to any of my former responsibilities. It was entirely gratifying.

I have received an occasional gratuity. I have also received some lovely perks, like the keys to the wine cellar, a maid, a man to take care of the pool, and the use of a grand piano in an acoustically well-designed room. These are wonderful surprises that various clients have been happy to share with me. Once you adjust your way of thinking to the old-fashioned bartering system, you then have loads of opportunities. Thus, money is never discussed during my negotiations. As you can see, I lead a tough life, but someone has to do it!

Building a Website

I do not consider myself a master of web building. There are many ways to approach the building of a web site. I used, perhaps, the lazy woman's way. Yahoo offers templates for building a web site through them. It was easy and looks great. Furthermore, I do believe my website is a useful tool.

My very first gig for Annie in England was done without the use of a website, proof that a good letter of introduction can be successful. I soon became interested though in making my house-sitting efforts as professional as possible. Feel free to take a look at www.housesit-pro.com at your convenience. Yahoo hosts this website for a small fee. I think it is worth it!

My website, Lean On Me International House Sitting, was not designed to accommodate the casual surfer. I suppose on occasions someone might stumble across it on their own surfing time. The purpose of the website, however, was to create an effective way to share information about myself with possible clients during our initial contact. I usually include the link in my first email.

My website is divided into eleven sections. I might have gotten a bit carried away when building the site, but it was a lot of fun. I have also always been a believer that too much information is better than not enough. At one point, I had a live video on my site, too. I took it off eventually because it became outdated, but I think that was an additional little touch that clients might have found interesting.

The eleven topics included on my site are the home page, a section listing the services that I can provide, a page about me, a page about my husband, information about confidentiality, a page talking about how I negotiate, testimonials, a photo gallery, updates about where I am in real time, and a list of unusual accomplishments. All of these pages do a pretty good job of giving a future client a clearer picture of who I am, what I have done, what I offer, and what they can do for me. Once again, I urge you to take the time to check out my web site in your spare time.

How to Find an Assignment

How do I go about locating the people who require a house sitter in an area of the world that I want to visit? It is simpler than one might suspect.

Fortunately, there are websites that serve as a kind of a middle man between those seeking an assignment and those in need of a house sitter. I have had success with several such web sites as Caretaker Gazette and Housecarers.com. These sites require membership and a small fee. It is a great way to locate lots of clients who are searching for someone to take care of their houses.

There are many different kinds of people who would like to have someone looking after things for them while they are away from home. The variety can be confusing. It makes sense to know in advance the parts of the world that you would like to visit and the length of stay that you would require as well. I am only interested in an assignment of no less than three weeks and no more than ninety days. Ninety days is often the longest that I am allowed to stay in many countries on my American passport. For me, I seek an area of outstanding natural beauty because I love nature and the wow factor that comes with certain regions of the world. I have lived cliffside at 1700 ft., overlooking the Caribbean in the Dutch Antilles. I have enjoyed the mountains in Andalucia, Spain. I have often been on an island or on coastlines. I am a dedicated walker. I usually require walking choices. I also prefer to have access to public transportation. I like smaller towns that provide the opportunity to take a bus or train to larger cities. At this time of my life, I am mostly interested in houses outside of the United States. I repeat all of the above simply because I fully understand that once a person starts sifting through the advertisements, it is easy to forget exactly what you previously decided upon as your dream job.

My needs may not be the same as yours. Once again, this is a question of preference. So, I urge all prospective house sitters, once again, to first decide in advance where they want to go and then what amenities they require in order to be comfortable. Once that is determined, the search for that perfect match can begin in earnest.

I got my first house through the Caretaker Gazette. It was perfect. Annie, the house owner, received about sixty letters of interest to the advertisement that she had placed with the Caretaker Gazette. It usually is competitive. Later, after we had settled that we actually were a good match, she confided that my letter of introduction stood out in some way to her from all the others that she received. I quickly learned that those letters of introduction can be as effective as a warm handshake and a smiling face can be. Take pains with writing the initial letter. Make it personal even if you have developed a template. First impressions do make all the difference!

Needless to say, a year is not a very long time. I have approached each of the last five years of my life a little differently. My traveling and living abroad has never been a full repeat of the preceding year. I design my life as I go along and as my personal needs change and dictate. However, a year is a pretty short time frame to fill with clients. Since I like to be out of the United States at least six to eight months each year, I usually need to find from two to four assignments. Remember, I can only stay about ninety days on my tourist passport in most countries. If I have two ninety-day gigs, I am set. You can see fairly easily that depending on personal preferences, you will not be spending too much time each year seeking a match. However, most folks will create their own model as not everyone will want to be gone from home as long as I have been each year.

Like anything in life, the getting started is often the trickiest part. Most people will not be as lucky as I was to get the very first job they applied to fill. Persistence will eventually pay off for those people who believe they have something to offer and know how to introduce themselves as well as negotiate for amenities successfully. Eventually, houses can even be recycled. I have returned to Spain many times. Why? I love Spain! That is my personal preference. I quickly discovered that Spain was in my top three favorite places in the world to live. Also, word of mouth can often open up new doors to new houses. If you have been highly successful with one client, they may recommend you to someone else. Annie recommended me to her relatives in France, for instance. Quickly, this whole thing begins to snowball......and surprisingly, you start to find yourself in a position to have to say no to some offers. After all, there are only twelve months in a year and only one little you to spread around. It is sweet to be in demand!

How to Negotiate

Oh, joy! You think you may have snagged a possible client! You have already defined your personal needs in regards to an assignment. You are able to articulate and write about your dream job. You have written a great introductory letter. You may have even built your web site. A client has responded to your letter with interest. What next?

I take my time with what comes next because I truly do believe that there are good matches and not so good matches between clients and house sitters. Thus far, I have never really had a poor match. I have had a few problems which I will discuss later, but those problems and their eventual solutions helped to fine tune my dream. The small lessons learned have since been added to my level of experience.

So do not hurry. Take the time to establish a dialogue. This can easily be done by an exchange of emails. Eventually, I do require a person to person phone conversation, but only if the arrangement appears to be promising. With the use of Skype, you can even use the web cam advantage and see your client face to face so to speak. They can pan the rooms in their house and gardens with the cam as well.

I provide references for all clients upon request. In the beginning, I used my old employers, the school district where I had served as a principal for many years. I do think my previous career served me well as for some reason or another teachers and principals are equated with good moral standing and a strong sense of responsibility, second only to nuns and ministers. Yet, I have no idea how many or if any clients for that matter called my old employers for a character reference.

Eventually, I acquired numerous personal recommendations from clients. They were always more than happy to write a recommendation and allowed me to post it on my web site. Everyone also agreed to accept a phone call from any new potential clients. Many referred me to friends and relatives, too. Once again, I do not know how many new clients ever placed a phone call to prior clients.

Most of my clients were a tad surprised that I wanted references from them as well. I usually asked for a reference from either an employer, a minister of the church they attended, or someone of some standing in the community. I did follow up on several, often by email. I still believe that if I am going to stay somewhere for many months that I need to know what I am getting myself into before I accept the gig. As I have already said, I have never really had a bad match to date.

When I reach the point where it looks like I have found a good match, a series of personal phone calls are very reassuring. After all, the client is entrusting their most precious assets to me, their home and often their animals. We both benefit from developing a bit of a relationship before they open their doors to me.

It becomes very important to be a good listener during this ongoing dialogue. Clients do not want to feel that you are only looking for a place to crash while you run off all day being a tourist. This is their home. They are nervous about leaving their cherished pets alone while they are gone for so long. They need to believe that this stranger that they are inviting into their home is trustworthy. They need to be able to go away for pleasure or business for an extended period of time and not worry about things back home. That is what we give them, peace of mind, utter peace of mind. They are so grateful for that! Once they are grateful, the future recommendations flow or the recycled houses become a reality. So practice good listening skills. Listen to all their needs and requests. Respond with good questions for clarification. Demonstrate an earnest interest in their pets and plants. Follow their requests to a tee.

Do not be eager to share your needs first. That will come in time. Remember, you are applying to work for them. After you have established exactly what they require, you can then share what you are looking for as well. Once this has been done and everyone is satisfied, you can then move to seal the deal.

My website is very helpful to clarify what I believe I bring to the job and what I require from the job as well. I usually include a link to my site in my introductory letter. That way, the client can read all about my prior career, my previous assignments, what I promise, what I require, my code of ethics, and even see pictures of me and some of my travels. It becomes a great springboard for our future dialogues.

I negotiate on an individual basis. If I want to go to a region badly enough, I will not always be a stickler for every little detail. For instance, I appreciate it if the client can provide me with a ride to and from the airport. Most have agreed. A few have been unable to do so because they were already absent from the home on my arrival. Usually, I have been picked up personally at the airport by the client or have had a taxi pick me up and paid for by the client. Occasionally, I have managed all on my own, but that is not my first choice and has been rare.

My web site www.housesit-pro.com is open for anyone to take a look at for helpful hints on how to put together a web site. I state on my web site that I agree to do roughly two hours of hands-on tasks as a house sitter. So, in addition to living on the premises and by so doing providing a measure of security to the property, I will perform, on request, the daily two-hour attention to designated chores. These tasks vary with each house. Walking a dog several times a day, watering plants, cleaning a litter box, feeding pets, collecting mail, and paying a few bills are fairly common. I have also cared for seedlings for a pair of sisters who were avid gardeners. I rotated the plants, fed them, watered them, monitored the grow lights, and started getting them accustomed to outdoor temperatures. The boat in Baja California required a few different tasks to be performed. I had to fill the water tanks on board and keep the decks clean. When my husband and I cared for the estate on the island of Saba, we had to pay attention to gardens and a pool. I have taken dogs to get their hair clipped and shampooed. I am open to many different kinds of tasks. I like to stay busy. However, if the client requires a lot of my time beyond the daily two hours, I then begin to negotiate for monetary compensation. That has been rare. I take great pride in returning the property to the hands of the owner in better condition than it was before I started the job.

I adore animals. Animals have always fallen head over paws for me, too. Ever since I was a kid, I have had a strong attachment to animals of all kinds. So for me to care for someone's pets is a treat. Annie's Manx cat, Charlie, was my baby on two different occasions. The last time I cared for Charlie, Annie knew that he was not in peak form. He was seventeen years old and failing. Charlie was Annie's baby. Charlie quickly became my baby, too. When his appetite was failing, I lovingly hand fed him. He actually gained a wee bit of weight while he was with me. Annie was less troubled about leaving him. She went to Italy reassured that he was being left in a safe and loving atmosphere.

Since many of my jobs have involved taking care of pets, I always let clients know how much I love animals. For many people, their animals are family. If they can go away and not feel guilty about leaving their furry family behind, they are forever grateful.

I have a keen respect for protecting the privacy of each client. I understand that allowing me to enter the sanctity of their home is a privilege. I do not ever abuse that privilege. I do not smoke and that is a bonus for the client. I also promise to not have anyone smoking on the property. I do not invite company to the house without first getting permission from the owner. Someone else's home should never become a crash pad for relatives and friends who would like to benefit from your good fortune by seeing Paris, for instance, on the cheap. I once asked permission from a client to have my daughter join me for a few days. Permission was granted. I have also once invited a friend to join me and use the guest house in Spain, but only after seeking permission from the owner of the house first. I cannot stress this enough. No house should ever become a hotel.

I promise to spend every night in the house. After all, the reason I am there is because the owner cannot look after their home while they have gone away. It does them no good to find that I have gone away, too. This has never been a problem for me. I am an untourist. I know I have repeated that a lot, but frankly, it is a prevailing attitude of mine that I think is essential to good house sitting. I have had several clients offer to let me stay on after their return so as to vacation a bit. I have never chosen to do so, but I am sure that there are clients that can be negotiated with easily on this count.

As far as the little extras in life that make my job easier, they usually materialize. I have never accepted an assignment where I was asked to cover any of the monthly bills, like the electric bill, for instance. I once was given a monthly food stipend on the island of Saba because food on the island was very expensive since it was all imported. That was very helpful. I have also had the use of cars on occasion. That is not usually a top priority of mine, because I generally take houses that have easy access to public transportation.

I have had some luxuries thrown my way as part of the package. More than once, I have had a housekeeper. I have also enjoyed several fine swimming pools. Other services that I have benefited from include gardeners, landscapers, and someone to attend to the pool.

Once, I oversaw the stripping and restoration of all the tile floors on the first floor of a fine home in San Miguel de Allende, Mexico. It was helpful that I could speak Spanish. It was also very convenient that I had an entire suite of rooms on the third floor, newly furnished just for me, with a personal balcony overlooking the entire city.

As you can see, my houses and families have varied quite a bit. That's why I negotiate individually. Each home is different. So, know what you offer, know where you want to be, listen to the owner's needs carefully, know what you need, check references, take the time needed to talk about things, deliver on your promises and more than likely you and the owner will both end up being very satisfied with the outcomes.

I have included a page from my site which suggests the kinds of services I can offer to a client. Of course, I remain open to additional suggestions from all clients. Knowing that I am a major animal lover and that all animals generally fall in love with me, I have felt very comfortable giving pets the extra care that their owners expect.

What can I do For You?

Tell me what you need before you leave your home. It is my goal to make your absence worry free!

What does a professional house sitter do?

A house sitter's job description is as varied as the individual client's needs.

Some benefits of having a professional house sitter include:

You can plan ahead

Your house will be more secure if someone is on the premises

While you are gone your pets can stay at home

Plants, gardens and yards can be maintained

Mail can be collected

Bills can be paid

Daily updates can be forwarded to you via emails or phone

Dehumidifiers can be operated

Your refrigerator can be stocked before you return

Allows for the gentle overseeing of other hired help

And much, much, more............................

What can you do for me?

Contact me

Let's see if we are a match

Determine a list of daily, weekly or occasional duties

Work out the details

Tell me how you will get me to and from the airport

I agree to approximately two hours each day of hands-on duties. Extra love for your pet is free, however!
I appreciate clear expectations. The more I know, the better I can serve you. So do not be shy. Specify!
I will consider all offers.

Having been a principal of an elementary school for many years, I understand the importance of confidentiality. Next is a page from my website about privacy issues.

Confidentiality
It is my promise that your home will remain your private domain.

I will treat your home with respect
I will treat your belongings with respect
I am a nonsmoker
I will not permit anyone to smoke on the premises
I will seek your permission before I invite anyone to visit me in your home
Your privacy will be guarded
All valuables will be protected
I will sleep on the premises every night
I will respect the neighbors
On your return you will find your home just the way you left it when you put it in my care
I will return all keys

I cannot stress enough how important maintaining a glowing reputation becomes to a successful house-sitting business. All you have is your reputation! If you fail to maintain total peace of mind for a client, you most definitely will not be asked to return. Having great letters of recommendations and folks who were pleased enough with your services to actually be willing to receive phone calls on your behalf from new clients seeking additional reassurance about you as a person is essential to securing good clients and plenty of opportunities.

The above promise that I included on my web site really defines my code of ethics in regard to protecting client confidentiality and privacy. Everyone's home is their castle. The kind of respect that I show to the homes and animals I care for is what makes all the difference. I am zealous about fulfilling my promises and guarding the sanctity of my client's personal domain.

How to Find Rentals

Originally, I stayed about nine months in Europe solely by living in rented properties. Eventually, I added the idea of taking care of homes to the scenario. I have also used rentals to fill in the gaps between jobs, especially if I am near a region that I would like to visit. Rentals can be very affordable during off season. The prices are also quite competitive if you can rent for a month or more at a time. There are many wonderful websites that feature what Europeans refer to as holiday houses. Often, landlords who have a holiday house will list their accommodations with these sites. They usually include multiple pictures of the interior and exterior of the place, a list of amenities, a calendar for bookings, other places of interest in the region, prices, and a means to contact the owner via email.

Most generally, these lovely homes and apartments are fully furnished and equipped for cooking and doing laundry. I usually choose several that would serve my purpose and send emails out to all, explaining that I am seeking a long term rental of a month or more and requesting the reduced rates offered for a lengthier stay. I have been pleasantly surprised with the responses. In Malta, I rented a gorgeous 400-year-old, stone house with inner courtyards and balconies, two bedrooms and marble staircases for the equivalent of $400 a month. The owner even picked us up from the airport on our arrival. We were able to live in this beautiful home for two and a half months. We shopped locally, did our own cooking in the fully equipped kitchen, and had access to buses that took us anywhere on the island for roughly seventy-five cents each way. That was a very affordable trip and remains to this day one of my favorite experiences.

Don't be afraid to dicker. Many of these places stand empty for part of the year. When an owner can fill the house for several months, they become very interested in negotiating. I have rented holiday houses in Prague, Ireland, Mexico, Spain, Malta, and Italy. If I had only been able to stay for a week or two, like most tourists, the prices probably would have been much, much more extravagant. I love a good deal. In order to take advantage of this kind of a deal, you must have plenty of time available to stay in these fine homes and apartments.

I can also say that the pictures on the websites of the houses that I have rented have almost always lived up to what I saw online. I do take the time before renting to ask any questions of the landlord that come to mind. In the end, I am generally pleased.

Which Do I Prefer?

I actually don't have a preference between being a house sitter and a renter. I enjoyed both. Each one has different pros and cons. They are really like comparing apples and oranges.

House assignments are economically a huge bang for your buck. For the cost of an airline ticket, you can stay in an area of the world of breathtaking beauty for months on end. There is virtually no overhead, once you get there. Many of the homes that I have stayed in were much more impressive than my own home in the United States. I also enjoy numerous amenities, depending on the gig. I have had maids, pool caretakers, and gardeners looking after things, while I merely keep some well-loved pet company. I have also benefited from having my wifi, telephone, heating bills, and even a stipend for groceries covered. It is a very low cost existence.

Of course, you are always aware that you are using other people's things and that your beloved stuff is far away. You may or may not have use of the family car. That is a personal choice of the owner. I have had cars at my disposal and I have done without and used public transportation. Usually, I am unable to travel on overnight trips while taking care of a home because the whole point of the job is to be there for the family pets or house security while the owner is gone. I do not mind, but that may not be the case for others. If you need or want to spend some time away from the house, occasionally, that could be cleared with the owner during the negotiation phase.

Rentals have a charm all of their own. You can be very specific about where you want to rent. For instance, I wanted to stay in Killarney and enjoy the great walking opportunities that the Killarney National Park offered. The two months in my Killarney rental were wonderful. Also, I was able to escape whenever I wanted by just locking the door, renting a car and driving away. I never did, but it was a choice that I had if I had wanted it.

Naturally, costs are higher for a renter than for a house sitter, but that is to be expected. I have been lucky to negotiate some wonderfully reasonable, long-term rentals that were all inclusive. I never hesitate to tack on a rental trip before or after an assignment if I can find a good rate. Also, traveling off season is a real cost saver. I like off season traveling because the crowds are greatly reduced. I do not limit my travel experiences to only certain seasons and weather. I have spent Christmas in Italy and Prague. I have also experienced the hottest part of the year in certain countries. It is all good!

Traveling Light

You are ready to go at last! I remember the feeling when I headed out on my very first job. I was excited, but nervous at the same time. I knew that I wanted to visit the region in England where I would be house sitting for almost a month, but I wondered if the house and the owners would be what I expected from the conversations and pictures that we had shared. All I can say is that I was not disappointed. Your first assignment is probably the most important in many ways. If you have a great experience, it will give you the courage to try again. If you do not have a good experience, it might bias you against the whole idea. I am not an easily discouraged person. No doubt, I would have tried again any way, but, fortunately, I was tickled with everything that transpired and the rest is history.

So let's talk a little bit about the travel process. How do you generally pack for a trip? It took me a few tries to understand that traveling light is cool. I packed far too much when I went abroad the first time. It was foolish now that I look back on it. I have learned from that experience though and have become a master packer. Most people are shocked when they see how little I bring with me.

Whether I am staying for ninety days or only a few weeks, the same tiny suitcase is my constant companion. I bought it from Walmart. It is really more like a backpack on wheels. It fits easily in an overhead bin of almost any airplane. I never check luggage as one of the things that can temporarily spoil a trip for me is lost luggage. If I have my bag with me at all times, I know that it will not be lost. Oh, I generally have a purse as well, but it is often emptied of contents and placed in the bottom of my suitcase for when I get to my destination.

How do I manage to travel so light? Well, I usually only bring around four outfits. I wear one pair of shoes and pack the other pair. I include very few toiletries because they can be purchased anywhere in the world. Yes, that is right! You can buy tooth paste, for instance, in Spain. I do not carry a laptop, no matter how small, because I have found that my little iPod Touch works like a charm. I have a voltage converter and a tiny soft case set of hot rollers. I have my camera. I sometimes have a swimsuit, but not always. I have three sets of underwear. If I have a sweater or a jacket, I wear it on the plane. I do not worry about possible, but unlikely, occasions when fine clothes would be necessary. I can buy a dress or nice shirt if I need one. I have my cell phone which I turn off and store once I leave the United States. While I am overseas, I seek out the wifi hot spots in restaurants, internet cafes, or in many cases the home where I am staying if it has internet service. I then use Skype on my iPod to place calls back to the United States. My Skype calls have always been clear as a bell and cost me nothing Skype to Skype and mere pennies Skype to land or cell phones.

If, later, there is anything that you decide that you need, you will be able to easily find it in any country that you visit. Chances are you will not need any particular items other than toiletries after you arrive though. I have on more than one occasion packed as light as described and still returned home with things that I never used. Less is more, my friends, less is more. The freedom that traveling light gives you is worth all of the tests that you find yourself putting each and every item through before it earns its rightful place among your things in that tiny suitcase. Leave the struggling with heavy, cumbersome bags and the disappointment of lost luggage to the fool! When you land at your final destination, you will grab your little suitcase from the overhead, skip off the plane, down the ramp and through the airport with hardly a care in the world.

Living Without a Car

There are a few Americans who can imagine living without a car, but not many. Frankly, the United States, for the most part, is not set up to easily accommodate the individual who does not want to be bothered with the ownership issues of a vehicle. Now I realize that even you, as my reader, are shaking your head right now and thinking you could never live without your chariot. Not only is a car pretty darn useful in the United States, but it is also a status symbol for many. Bear with me though for just a few more minutes. I want to just give you a couple of things to think about it.

I ask you to remember first of all that if you use my model for world travels, you will not be traveling large distance after your arrival. You will instead be lavishing yourself with long, sultry afternoons in a local café of some adorable old-world town where you have chosen to set up housekeeping. That changes things immensely. The point being that you will not be traveling much farther than the distance you can go in a day, returning to your house the same night.

During our first year abroad, we only rented a car on two different weekends while we were in Ireland. We did not rent a car during our three months in Spain. We did not rent a car in Malta. In fact, in all of our travels, the six days in Ireland remain the only time that we have ever felt we wanted to break our "no rent a car rule". We have used taxis quite a bit. Taxis were wonderful options, especially in Malta and Mexico because they were quite inexpensive. We could get all around San Miguel de Allende for a few dollars each way. We have used trains, another wonderful transportation option. Of course, buses tend to be a first choice and often the most affordable. Any way you look at it, all options, when used wisely, are less expensive than a long-term car rental.

Our daily lives were filled with walking, a lot. In fact, we were such good walkers, much to our surprise, that we lost weight and toned up without even trying to do so. That was a nice secondary benefit. When we did not feel like walking or the weather was too lousy or the distance too great, we used public transportation. We missed having these choices when we came back to the United States.

The money that one can save by not owning a car is significant. Just think.....no gas bills, no insurance payments, no repairs, or no high cost of renting a vehicle. It really can become a nuisance. A car is a luxury, but also a financial burden.

Occasionally, one of our amenities with an assignment was the use of the family car. I used a car in Cape Cod. I also was privy to a car of sorts, an old beat up island vehicle on the Isle of Saba in the Dutch Antilles. I will be returning to Spain soon and will have use of a car once again.

Of course, if not having a car will spoil your good time by all means indulge yourself with a car rental. I, nonetheless, found that living abroad without a car was so doable and so much less expensive that I actually resented having to return to the world of car dependency when I went home.

Windmill in Ireland

Typical street in Competa, Spain

City of Prague

Pool on 1700 ft. cliff at our house on the isle of Saba

Our house in Ireland

Blue Grotto sea caves on Malta.

View of Competa, Spain

Looking to the sea from Valletta, Malta

Language Barriers

Please do not allow a language barrier to determine whether or not you would consider including any country on your list of places you must see. I have spent lots of time in countries that do not speak English and have found that there is always a way to communicate with the natives. Most people are eager to help out. With a little imagination, you can find ways to get your point across. It has also been my experience that there are more people who speak a smattering of English, even a lot of English, in other countries than there are people in the United States who speak enough of a second language to accommodate foreign travelers who come here.

I am proficient in a second language, Spanish. This makes it a little easier also to understand some Italian, French, and Portuguese. If you think that you are going to gravitate toward a group of countries that speak a particular language, consider learning some of the language ahead of time and then actively adding to your language skills while living abroad. There is no better way to acquire a second language than in the country of its origin. Furthermore, I have been told that learning a second language can stimulate the brain in such a way as to save those little grey cells that most of us as we are aging, are fearful of losing. Enjoy the challenge!

Unexpected Problems

I am a practical woman. I have the capacity to dream and imagine, but before I wander off to chase my dreams, I apply some very sound calculations. I accept the fact that there is a strong probability that at one time or another while I am living abroad that I will encounter some problems. That is life! That is life abroad or at home. I must be prepared for the unexpected.

I do not allow a problem to alter my enthusiasm about life abroad. I have generally realized that most things in life are not an emergency. I try to conserve my energy for the true emergencies in life. Many things can appear to be dire at first and can cause enough anxiety when viewed as another emergency to spoil a whole day, week, or longer if we so choose. Most of the time, after everything has been resolved, we realize that the worst that was imagined never came to pass and that the problem almost solved itself if we managed to remain calm.

Living abroad for me is no different than living at home. I am, after all, just going about my business of living. There are no big differences. I eat, I cook, I entertain myself, I make friends just as I would in the United States. Having said all of this, I will now share some of the unexpected problems that have come my way while living abroad.

Surprisingly, during the past years of traipsing all over the world, I have had nothing happen that could be considered a true emergency. Some of the things that have happened were resolved in an unexpected fashion though.

One problem that was resolved in a most unexpected manner took place in Malta. At this time, we were renting a holiday house. We really liked Malta a lot. Part of our daily routine usually involved walking to the nearest grocery store to purchase what we needed for the meal of the day. My husband and I both love browsing in foreign grocery stores. This particular walk turned out to be a bit traumatic as on that day he insisted on carrying money, credit cards, and passports in a money belt worn under his shirt. He did not realize that the money belt had fallen off on our way back to the house. Needless to say, when the discovery was made, panic prevailed. I admit it, I joined in the panic mode, too. I was rather a novice still at this living abroad thing. It seemed that everything that we had in that single money belt was of great importance to our life abroad.

We had no phone at the time, but needed to call and cancel our credit cards. So I decided to pay a visit to the local parish priest who lived around the corner from us. He took us to the town office down the street and they were kind enough to allow us to call our bank. What we would do without a card for our use would have to be figured out later. Next, we went to the United States Embassy. We took a bus there, buses were abundant and cheap. We received the papers to apply for a new passport. By this time, we were exhausted. We had worn ourselves out by remaining in an emotional state of emergency. We were downhearted as we headed back to our house.

When we arrived back home, there was a note on our door. It appeared that a lovely man had found our money belt and carried it home with him. On inspection, he found a slip of paper with our names and the address of the house where we were living. We usually carried the address with us which turned out to be a good idea. His most welcome note said that he had our things at his house and would we care to come around and collect them. He included his address which was only a few blocks from our house. We were ecstatic! We headed there immediately and were received by this kind man who did, indeed, hand everything over to us. We were so grateful to him. It is always reassuring to find out that there are wonderfully kind and honest people living all over the world. Oh, by the way, we returned to the town hall to call our credit card service, canceling the prior cancellation of our cards. The day was saved. We were back in business!

We had a camera lifted from our backpack in Prague. We were on the tram and there were signs posted saying to beware of pickpockets. Well, they were right! We had to buy another camera while we were there. At the time, I was unwilling to sacrifice photo memories. However, the more that I have traveled the less that I feel compelled to capture so many memories on camera. These memories are so uniquely personal that a picture does not really do them justice. Also, there comes a point when trying to share the hundreds of pictures with people becomes ludicrous.

I was burgled in Ajijic, Mexico. A few dollars in my purse and some money on the bedside table that I was to give to the gardener were the extent of my losses. The experience itself was a bit harrowing. It always must be when you find out that someone has entered your sanctuary and rifled through your things, but I also know that this could have happened to me back home just as easily. I did not let it bother me too much.

I got sick in Malta. The problem being that it was only a few days before my departure. I was afraid that I would not be able to fly. I went to a local doctor and he saw me without an appointment. He was very kind. He gave me some medicine. After struggling with how much to charge me, Malta has socialized medicine, we settled on fourteen dollars. I was fit to fly by departure time!

I had one pet, a pretty Mexican street dog, that had been adopted by my client and still had a number of old, bad habits that I had to contend with before I finally figured out that crating the dog was the only way that Brownie could be secure enough to be left alone in the house while I went out. I do always promise to spend every night on the premises of the house that I am caring for, but I still go places during the day. Brownie was already extremely anxious about his master being gone. The separation anxiety caused some old behaviors to return in full force. Brownie had had a very neglected and abused life prior to adoption. I quickly realized that when left alone he could be very destructive, chewing furniture and belongings. After two separate incidents of this type, I contacted his owner by email. They immediately responded with surprise and concern. They had believed that Brownie no longer would behave this way and had failed to tell me the location of the dog crate for such situations. Once Brownie and I had established that I would continue to leave the house regularly while he stayed in his crate, things ran smoothly.

There will be problems. Whether I stay home in the United States or live abroad, shit happens. That is the way of life. A proper attitude can go a long way toward determining just how extreme the problem really is and how much time the problem actually consumes. Stay cool whenever possible!

Health Insurance

I retired earlier than most. I was fifty-four and a good ten years away from being able to receive Medicare. So I had to be a little creative about health insurance. There are several ways to look at this little dilemma. If you are going to be out of the country for at least six months every year, you may want to consider some sort of global health insurance. This type of insurance is often purchased by expatriates. I carried it for a while. It was pretty affordable and the beauty of the plan is that it covered me everywhere in the world, even in the United States. Many people are surprised when I add the little phrase "even in the United States", but that part is the trickiest. Why? Health care in the United States is expensive, the most expensive in the world. Paying for expensive health care out of pocket can drain your resources quickly. However, many of the global plans are much more affordable. Why, you ask again? These American companies have a large client base. They count on many of their clients to receive health care in the foreign country where they are currently living. At the end of the day, the more clients that are consulting with foreign doctors or receiving treatment in hospitals outside of the United States, the cheaper it will be for everybody. Therefore, the company can offer a plan that is hundreds of dollars less expensive than usual. The hitch is that you must be out of the country at least six months each year. It does not have to be six consecutive months though.

If you are eligible for Medicare or you are only out of the country for a few months or weeks at a time, you may want to consider travel insurance which can often be purchased as an add on to your air expenses. There are also companies who specialize in travel insurance. The concept of travel insurance is that you would only be carrying it to cover true emergencies. It is comforting to have it though and could come in handy.

Stay Out of Debt

I am now going to write a few paragraphs about something that I believe is extremely fundamental to my ability not just to travel, but to live a free and unencumbered life! I stay out of debt! I have been in debt. I have been without debts. I can tell you from personal experience that no one is ever free if they are in debt. In fact, I believe so firmly that being debt free is the only way to live my life that I do everything in my power to not be seduced back into the world of indebtedness.

How does it happen anyway that intelligent people with an adequate income can find that they are drowning in debt? I am not much of a conspiracy theorist, but I am tempted to believe that in this case there is a master plan afoot that operates on the principle that if people can be convinced to buy things that they really cannot afford, then they will be enslaved to the system for many years to come. How are people convinced to sell their freedom for the price of a snazzy car or a few luxury items? They are first of all encouraged to believe that these items are essential to their happiness or to the level of status they want to portray. Next, they are led to believe that they can have anything they desire just as long as they can make the payments. Once the debt cycle begins, it becomes a ruthless game of robbing Peter to pay Paul in order to acquire the endless array of items that suddenly seem desirable. Desire is a bitch! It can drive a person headlong into misery.

You may be shaking your head again and thinking that I am too radical about these matters. The ability to live without incurring debt has been the single most positive thing that I practice in my new lifestyle. Even if I stayed home and never traveled again, I would reap huge benefits by not allowing myself to get in debt. If you are not out of debt already, you may want to start getting yourself positioned for a new life down the road, a life that affords peace of mind as well as a little left-over cash in your pocket. You will then be free at last to live the life that you are really longing to live.

I Have Shared All of My Secrets

Well, now you know everything that I know. Maybe not everything, but I have shared a lot of details about my little travel business with you. Yet, there is one thing I cannot give you. I cannot hand you any experiences. That is something that we all must acquire on our own time.

If I have learned anything at all in my almost sixty years on this planet, it is that dreaming is a wonderful way to pass the time. I am all for dreaming. When we lose our ability to dream and imagine, we lose so many possible options in life. I love to dream. Many of my wildest dreams have come true.

I am definitely a dreamer at heart, but I also understand that while dreams are good, a considerable amount of dream chasing is necessary to see a dream become a reality. If you have a dream, go after it. If you have stopped dreaming, start again. Do not let anyone convince you otherwise.

My dream is now part of my life. Although it does not play out the same way every year, it is always a variation on the theme of international travel. Being a house sitter is an important piece of what makes my dream doable. It is not the only way that I travel and live abroad, but it is by far the least expensive. I will continue to tinker with this lifestyle, hoping with each experience to improve upon the process.

Recently, I returned to Spain to care for the home of my good friend Katherine. She and her husband Ian went to Australia to visit their daughter and grandchildren. They were kind enough to ask me to take care of the house and cats while they were gone. I jumped at the chance!

I keep a journal while traveling. I kept a journal on this trip, too. Journaling is a great way to manage all the memories that I have created for myself. Someday, long after I am gone, my little granddaughter might read my journal. She will be surprised, I hope, by the many wonderful adventures that her Gram experienced. For now, though, I choose to share a small section of my personal journal with my readers. Twenty-two days in Spain is not a very long time, but they were days of pure joy. It is my wish that anyone who reads the following journal will recognize the peace of mind and the tranquility of soul that I experienced on this particular occasion. It should also further clarify how quiet and often uneventful my living abroad can be. The key to it all is in the living not the doing. I live in areas of outstanding natural beauty, all over the world. When anyone asks me what I do while I am there, this journal is a good example.

THE JOURNAL

Day 1

Although I safely arrived in Spain five days ago, this morning is my first official day of house sitting. At about 7 AM, I saw Katherine and Ian off to the Malaga airport. I was pleased to see that they felt comfortable knowing that their house, gardens, and five well-loved cats would be safe in my capable hands. So, as they head to Australia to see their grandchildren, they can do it free of worry.

One of the perks of traveling the way I do is that you make loads of friends along the way. I have collected good friends all over the world. Katherine and Ian are at the top of my list. They are two lovely retired Brits who having first seen a lot of the world, settled upon village life in the mountains of Andalucia, Spain as their retirement home. What a choice, too!!!!! They live just a couple of kilometers outside the village of Competa in el campo (the country). Spreading out below their lovely house and gardens are the mountains and valleys of the Almijaras and even larger mountains looming above them serve as a backdrop to their life. The Mediterranean Sea can be viewed from the windows of the house, all of the patios, and the pool. On a very clear day the Moroccan coastline appears like a delicate etching on the horizon. The little village of Corumbella hangs on the mountainside across the valley, snowy white in the Andalucian sun, against the blue sky, and sparkling with lights in the night air. They have a small modern home, built largely in the Andalucian fashion, with gorgeous gardens surrounding, climbing, and embracing the four patios and pool.

Daily life at Katherine's house is a spiritual experience. It meets one very important requirement of mine. This is, indeed, an area of outstanding natural beauty! I can be content with long hours of solitude while sipping tea or a glass of wine and gazing out across the panoramic views afforded me. In this reflective mood, life seems sweeter than usual. I am able to find my center and appreciate the beautiful world that has always been there for me to enjoy, except that now I have the time to actually partake of its splendor. I do not take for granted what I see, hear, smell, taste or touch.

Yet, this particular house is special in one other very important way. I do not need to be alone for long if I decide I want or require companionship. This is my fourth time to live in this area and, therefore, I have many friends and acquaintances living in and around the village. By the time that I have finished caring for this house, I will have lived in the Competa area for a total of seven months. It is a place that lures me back over and over again.

Coming back to Competa feels like going home. Competa is 700 meters above sea level in the Sierra Almijaras. These mountains stretch between Malaga and Granada and to the warm Mediterranean Sea. It is a midsized village surrounded by a wildlife reserve, with peaks as high as 2068 meters. Many people come to this region to walk the paths that wind around and up the mountains in this stunningly beautiful area of Spain. Yet, the sandy beaches and gorgeous coastal towns are very near as well.

With that backdrop, I can settle in today, knowing that what I seek all over the world, the peace and grandeur of nature, is mine for the next sixteen days. I had a lot of fun during the five days leading up to Kat's departure. When she picked me up at the airport, we drove the coastal route to Torre Del Mar, where we ascended to the village high above us. On our way, Katherine treated me to my very first cup of Spanish coffee in a beachside cafe. This is no small treat if you are a coffee lover.

Each day that we drove her small car into Competa, I invariably bumped into old friends. It was fun to see the look of surprise on their faces. Most of my friends did not know that I was coming to Spain. It is nice to be liked though!

One day when I am writing in my journal, I will describe in detail our evening at La Roca when the Spaniards performed flamenco music and danced for us, but not today. Today is reserved for the beauty of solitude. Basking in the warm sun, I will wash my travel clothes and hang them to dry in the mountain air. I will also strip Katherine´s bed and wash and dry her sheets and duvet for when she returns. Those little touches are always appreciated when a house owner comes home after a long trip.

Tomorrow I will venture out in the little car and test my ability to drive these winding mountain roads. That will be an experience, to say the least, as up until now, I have never driven a car while in Spain. A good challenge is always welcome! It keeps me from growing lazy.

It is almost full moon. I will stay awake tonight to see the spectacle of a luminous moon bathing the mountains with light. As far as I'm concerned, it doesn't get much better than this!

Day 2

It is just another beautiful day in paradise! I was shocked when I woke up to find that I had slept until 9:30. Yikes! My plans had been to rise much earlier, shower, feed the cats, and drive to town before it got too hot. Well, so much for well-made plans. I simply skipped the shower.

I do not totally ignore a schedule, but I also do not have a lot of rules in my life these days. After reporting to school for my whole life, from age five to age fifty-four, I now prefer to go with the flow. And, yes, I was in school all those years, either as a student or an educator. I still can be very organized. If I make a promise, I get it done, but one of my personal joys about not doing traditional work any more is that I now have so much more flexibility.

So let me talk about driving in this region. This is a first for me! Before, when I was in Spain, I lived in the village and had no need of a car. I could walk anywhere in Competa without difficulty. Mind you, walking in Competa is not for the lazy. Everything is largely straight up or straight down. The first time I was here, I was recuperating from a broken knee. After three months managing the steep streets of the village, my knee was operating normally at last. For whatever reason, these strenuous streets were just what the doctor ordered to restore and rebuild the muscles that controlled my knee cap. Since then, I have always told people that I went to Spain the first time for my health, returning to the United States totally renewed. But in all actuality, it was a unexpected benefit.

Nevertheless, if walking is a challenge, then it might be fair to say that driving requires a mixture of death defying skill and sheer courage, tinged by an element of stupidity for even making the effort. Katherine, bless her heart, left her little orange Fiat for me to use. She has lived here for roughly eight years and zips around as she pleases. I, on the other hand, never having loved to drive in the first place, have had to screw up as much courage as possible to even take the car out of the driveway. I have this theory that fear must be overcome or else it will swallow you whole.

There are two tracks to Competa. One is along the ridge and eventually enters the middle part of Competa. The other is on the main road, entering the bottom of Competa. They are both scary as hell to me. The first one seems to have less traffic, but the road is quite narrow and there are places where only a single vehicle could pass with ease. Backing up would be one thing, but backing up on a winding path that hangs on the side of a steep ravine is quite another thing altogether. The second route has more traffic coming up the mountain from the coast, including trucks making deliveries and buses carrying people. I go as slow as is permitted, but those switchbacks are harrowing, and meeting a truck as I take a sharp curve is totally unacceptable. Often, they are not completely on their side of the road. The Spanish have a tendency to go faster than I think is wise. The expats are often retired folks, many of whom should not be driving in their own home countries let alone in the Almijara Mountains of

Spain. I took the first route this morning and lived to write about it tonight.

I have a number of house tasks to perform as usual. Essentially, I am caring for five cats, a pool, and the potted plants. The five cats live outside, although they are allowed to enter the sun porch if they take a notion. Ian grumbles about the cats. Katherine only had four cats the last time I was here, but Pongo has adopted the Patersons since then. Katherine has a soft heart and has taken in stray cats that are in desperate need of food and care. She has a good relationship with the local veterinarian, who, no doubt, appreciates her business. I like to tease her by saying that poor cats choose to join her menagerie because they know that they will receive free health care. Since I am an American and Katherine is English, we both think the joke is funny.

In addition to feeding and watering the cats twice a day, I also provide them with company and TLC, which they appreciate. How do I know? They follow me around the property wherever I go. What can I say? Animals love me.

Every third day, I water the many, many potted plants that reside on the four patios. It takes me about 45 minutes to thoroughly water these beauties. All the plants that are planted directly in the ground do not get watered, except for a few new plants that are not fully established. Before I water the plants, I fill the pool. This requires very little effort on my part, but once I put the hose in the pool, I have to remember to return in about an hour or so to check the level. When these two tasks are completed, I am finished for another three days.

I like the outdoor work. It keeps me from just sitting and rotting. It is warm and sunny with rarely ever a cloud to mar the blue skies. The views are breathtaking. The cats keep me company. If my husband were caring for this house with me, it would take even less time to do these few chores. This time I am on my own, however, and fortunately, I enjoy it either way. We have a good time together, but frankly, I am endlessly fascinated with my own company. I can be alone, but I am never lonely.

Day 3

I spent the whole morning in the village! I started with my morning coffee and a lovely breakfast in the plaza at La Casona, followed by a long, leisurely chat with my friend Ursula. It has been almost two years since I have been here, so there is a lot of catching up to do with many different people.

Ursula is a German expat who prior to coming to Spain lived in England for many years. Her English is excellent. I like Ursula. Just like me, she is an independent woman. She does not quite fit into any particular box or category. I have often described myself as a "citizen of the world". I stole that from Thomas Paine, but identified with the phrase from the first time I read it on a plaque in Lewes, England. I think I could be happy living in many parts of the world. So far, that has been proven to be literally true. As is often the case in small villages, one thing leads to another. It would appear that I may be going to the coast tomorrow with Ursula to visit May Doris, a mutual friend of ours from Scotland, who now lives in the lovely, seaside town of Nerja. I will phone Ursula later this evening to confirm the plans.

Katherine and Ian are safely in Australia, tired, but head over heels in love with the sight of their two grandchildren. This is a sentimental state that can only be appreciated by other grandparents. Believe me, I know, because my little granddaughter has the power to keep her Omi off the road these days in a way that no one else can do. Even as I write these lines, I miss her.

I have not figured out a way to be in two places at once yet. I wish I could, though. I have a small dilemma at the moment. I received an unexpected email from Charlotte and Mary in Cape Cod. They are going to make a trip to China in the fall and are seeking my services again. I am very tempted, but I have already made plans to go to San Miguel de Allende in the fall. This will have to sort itself out.

I have been eating and enjoying the lovely Jamon Serrano, which is a kind of Spanish ham that is sort of like prosciutto. I also have been nibbling on Spanish olives. My meals at home are simple, good bread, ham, cheese, a little wine, and fresh fruit. A Spanish neighbor has promised to bring me fresh figs soon.

Competa is situated on the Costa del Sol which boasts of having one of the best climates in Europe. The land that surrounds the village is filled with vineyards, olive, almond and lemon orchards, and tropical fruits such as avocado, mango and kiwi. All are ideally suited to this subtropical climate. The region is famous for the small whitewashed villages and farm houses. This is where the muscatel grapes are grown and harvested. The Vino de Competa, the local wine, is made from the muscatel grapes. The Mediterranean diet is one of my favorites.

DAY 4

I suppose it is important to remember that even paradise had a serpent that did the dirty deed, spoiling things for Adam and Eve. I am fully aware of the problems that can present when abroad. I have had my share of things to solve. I also know that whether in Spain or at home, there will be the occasional problem. Most problems can be solved without a reaction involving hysterics from me.

Yesterday evening, I was standing at the edge of the garden that overlooks the valley and the little village of Corumbella when Pongo, the latest addition to the cat menagerie, merely started rubbing up against my legs, as cats will do. This act was totally uninvited. I was surprised. I understood that the cat was wild and horribly neglected before it adopted Katherine and Ian. Although it is now fed regularly and has been accepted into the family, it suffers a mild social disorder. Pongo can be unreliable, occasionally swatting, hissing and even biting for no apparent reason. So, I was surprised at the display of affection and merely stood very still until Pongo had completed his ritual. He then stretched out on the ground beside me. I made no effort to pet him. I did not want to spook him. As I took my first step to walk away, the cheeky little bastard bit me. I was shocked! I immediately went inside to examine the bite. It was a single puncture wound, drawing only two, itsy, bitsy drops of blood, but I was uncomfortably aware that the breaking of skin was probably not a good thing.

Here is the new learning that I have gained from this experience. Everyone should probably make sure they know when they got their last tetanus shot. I thought that my last one was still within the ten year limit, but I could not be certain. I called Inge, a wise and caring German woman of 80 plus years. She advised me to see the doctor at the village clinic the next morning. Interestingly, any expat I talked to urged me to see the doctor, whereas, the Spanish I talked to seemed surprised that I was making such a fuss. I couldn't help but recall the old days when I was a kid. Going to the doctor back then was a rare thing. Somehow I survived my careless upbringing. However, being a cautious American, when it comes to the horrors of medical complications, I went to the doctor.

It is on these occasions that technical terms are noticeably lacking from my Spanish vocabulary. I spent a few minutes looking up some key words on my translation application that I had downloaded onto my iPod. Off I went then to attempt medical consultation.

Three things transpired. I was given a tetanus shot, none too gently. I was given a prescription for antibiotic creams. Apparently, I also confused the doctor and the receptionist with my travel insurance. This is the second time in all of my travels that I have had to seek a doctor's care. Both times, they had no idea what to charge me or what to do with my insurance. My Spanish doctor said that they would send the bill to me after my return to the United States. I could then submit it to the insurance company. I was prepared to pay the bill up front, collect the receipts, and later submit it if the bill exceeded $50, which was my deductible. I sincerely doubt if I ever get a bill, but if I do I will gladly submit it.

After spending the greater part of a day dealing with the doctor, the prescription and so forth and so on, I was tired and returned to the house to take a nap and clean up for the evening. I had been invited to join Sandra, Ursula, and Magney at their reserved table in the plaza for a world cup game featuring Spain versus Chile. Futbol!

To understand the sheer madness in the larger part of the world surrounding futbol, and most definitely in the whole of Europe, one really must be present somewhere other than the United States during the World Cup. I have been present in Spain on two such occasions. I must say that there are three things that do not particularly excite me in life, politics, religion, and sports. I have never been infected with the fever that infects fans of these three very important social practices. Yet, I have enjoyed watching the eclectic group of people from so many different countries gather in the plaza to watch the games. They seemed to cheer for their home countries individually, but collectively cheered for Spain.

DAY 5

What a pleasant day! As usual the weather consisted of nothing but sunshine. The climate in southern Spain is similar to southern California. The winter brings cooler temperatures and rain. The rest of the year is sunny, warm, and dry. The lack of humidity makes the heat tolerable. Generally, during the months of July, August, and September, the afternoon heat can be quite daunting, but the Spanish have good sense and essentially stay indoors until the sun starts to set and the evening coolness arrives. It is advisable to go out during the morning and run your errands. Many of the shops close for the afternoon and reopen later to avoid the heat. The weather, since I have arrived, has been glorious, temperature highs not exceeding 85 degrees, and the nights are cool enough to require a light blanket.

After a late night of futbol in the village square, I elected to spend the entire day at home. It was a peaceful day. I did two loads of laundry and hung them out to dry in the courtyard. I skimmed and filled the pool. I watered all of the plants. I spent time with the cats. They seem to enjoy my company, even the little bastard who bit me, but, of course, I do not give him the benefit of the doubt.

I use Skype. I actually use Skype even when I am at home in the United States, but it is particularly handy when I am abroad. If I have access to the internet, I can call any friends or family members back home. I bought a universal telephone number from Skype. It is a stateside telephone number. It costs me $30 a year. Now, everyone can also call directly to my computer or iPod from their cell phones or land phones as though it is a domestic phone call. That is very helpful and cheap! Of course, Skype to Skype is totally free. I even have Skype downloaded onto my iPod. I can use my iPod as an international cell phone as long as I have access to wifi. Lots of cafes have public wifi these days, so I make a point, when I am in a town, to locate these convenient spots. I do love modern technology!

Today, thanks to Skype, I called a lot of people back home and caught up on things. It was fun! I always miss my family when I am gone and the joy of talking on the phone and seeing their faces at the same time brings me great pleasure.

All in all, the day has gone by quickly. In fact, my time is slipping by much faster than I had anticipated. This is a short assignment. I could have taken care of Katherine's house until mid August, which would have been about eight weeks total, but, until my little granddaughter is at least a year old, I have altered my schedule to being gone no more than a month at a time. So, I will return and play with her for several months before I go abroad again.

DAY 6

One sunny day after another is pretty darn nice! I passed a lovely morning at Casa La Colina. That is the name of Katherine's house. No time-consuming chores required my attention. Except for feeding the cats, I spent the morning just puttering. I am good at puttering.

I had been invited to meet Magney and Ursula in the plaza for the big game of the day between England and Germany. I decided to go into the village a bit earlier in order to first eat a proper meal at La Casona, which is one of two cafe/bars located on the plaza with outdoor seating under large sun umbrellas. They and the next door cafe have set up three large-screened televisions so that people can eat, drink and watch futbol.

I had a lovely meal. Unlike many people who find eating alone at a restaurant uncomfortable, I have absolutely no problem with it at all. In fact, although I have been married all of my life, forty years recently, I have discovered that when I travel alone, I do very well on my own. Since I am an independent woman who earns her own money and pays her own way in life, I now also know that I can achieve a lovely quality of life while living completely on my own. Dining out alone is no exception.

I make an attempt to treat myself well when traveling alone. If cooking at home, I try to lavish myself with my favorite foods and lovely wines. I set the table as though I am receiving company. I keep lots of gorgeous fresh fruit in the house. Right now I am enjoying las sandias, watermelons, that are currently in season and absolutely divine.

My favorite music is never far away, because I usually carry my iPod Touch with me. That handy little device keeps all of my essentials readily available. I can check my emails, send emails, surf the net looking for answers to my questions, read books, use Skype, listen to my favorite tunes, translate English to another language and more. The iPod is the equivalent to a modern-day Swiss Army Knife. I even have a flashlight application that comes in handy from time to time.

Getting back to my afternoon in the plaza, I enjoyed a leisurely meal topped off with Spanish coffee before my friends arrived. I even got asked out. I am not bragging, but apparently men still find me attractive, even though I am almost sixty years old. A Dutchman approached me from another table as he got up to leave. He had been eyeing me appreciatively for over an hour. I kid you not when I say that he had to be almost 80 if he was a day. His English was poor. He approached me and said, “Can I ask you a question?” I thought to myself, well sir, you just did, but I said out loud, instead, and politely, “yes, of course.” Americans are so afraid of being unfriendly, you know. He then attempted to show and tell me that he had tobacco and a newspaper, so would I like to accompany him to another bar. Although the offer was tempting, I do not smoke and rarely read the paper, my philosophy being that news has very little to do with me. The less I know the happier I am. So I declined the offer politely, once again. He was a perfect gentleman and left without putting up a fight.

My friends arrived as promised and we commenced watching the game. As I have already said, I am not particularly into sports of any kind. I guess I am not a very good team player. I live without borders. I do not root for any particular team or government or religion. It is not something that I do to annoy or offend. It is simply that I have adopted a very individualistic philosophy to life. I used to say that I was a citizen of the world, but recently I have started to say that I am actually a citizen of an alternate universe. I live in my own little world and find it to be quite pleasant. I discriminate, but only against mean people. Mean people scare me. I avoid them. Incidentally, I have discovered that there are mean people all over the world. I also have discovered a lot of lovely people all over the world. People are largely the same no matter where you are living.

The games went well, I guess. The conversation was nice. The breeze was spectacular. I passed away another pleasant afternoon among friends and acquaintances to return to my house once again to watch the sun set over the Almijara mountains. By the way, Germany won!

DAY 7

I have managed to find ways to spend another beautiful day alone at Casa La Colina. I enjoy my alone time in this beautiful location, so I am careful to have a nice mix of social activities and solitude. Even as a child, I required a major portion of alone time, time set aside just to be me, to think my own thoughts and to relax. I am rarely lonely. I know how to be alone, but not lonely. I am endlessly fascinated with my own company, and the older I get the more content I become, the more comfortable I feel in my own skin. I do believe that I am my own best friend. Having said that, I must admit that my social calendar is far more hectic in this little Spanish village than it is back home. I know so many people in the village. Many invite me to dinner in their homes or for coffees in the plaza. Not all of the places that I go to are quite like this, but I function happily either way.

I went into the village for about an hour and a half today to have my coffee at Cafe Competa at the bottom of the village. I also collected the mail. Katherine and Ian had intended to leave an emergency fund of money with me and in the rush of getting packed and out the door on the day of their departure, they simply forgot. They ended up mailing the money to me from the London airport. I was happy to retrieve it today.

Lastly, I went to the grocery store to buy a few items. My food bill has been very low since my arrival. Katherine had a lot of stuff in the house already and instructed me to use anything and everything that I wanted. An emergency fund and packed larders are both very common perks with an assignment. In fact, unless there is an arrangement with the owner to contact a friend or relative in case of an emergency, the stash of cash is necessary, especially for unexpected vet bills. At any rate, I brought 365 Euros with me. Even though I treated Ian and Katherine to a meal at El Museo, I still have 125 euros left. I feel like I have been freely spending money. I eat out when I want, usually lunch or breakfast, buy my coffees, buy my drinks, and buy groceries and personal items. I even purchased a pair of earrings for myself, which is a rare occurrence. I also bought a child´s flamenco dress for Lilly. I have to admit, I am not a big spender by most people's standards. I have never been very materialistic. Material things are nice, but whenever I have had extra money in the past, I have applied it to travel. I prefer experiences to collecting stuff.

I generally do not purchase souvenirs or extras to bring back with me. My husband and I made a pact with each other after we downsized from our house in Maine. We agreed to never acquire so much stuff again. One downsizing experience was enough for us.

I compete with myself every time I get ready for another trip. How can I beat my travel light record? It is impossible to truly travel light if one is constantly buying items to take back with them. My little suitcase on wheels is 22 inches and fits the overhead bins perfectly. Thus, everything that goes into it must be judged a "suitcase-worthy" item first. I do not check a second suitcase. The compulsion to add things to my suitcase has been overcome. I watch other people with their giant suitcases and extra bags and bundles, and I cringe with their discomfort. That is a ridiculous way to travel. I carry my iPod touch instead of a laptop computer. I am considering the iPad because it has a larger screen size, but still weighs only a little over a pound, but for the time being, I am not convinced that it would be better than my handy little iPod.

I am a night owl, so as the Spanish sun sets every evening, I generally start to close up the house and settle in for a quiet time of reading, writing, watching television, catching up on emails, and making phone calls because of the six hour time difference. Well, there is a six hour time difference with my husband and son and family, but nine hours with my daughter in California. Katherine and Ian are many hours different in the opposite direction. It can get a little confusing at times. It does not get truly dark here until almost 10 PM, but the after-hour time has always been a good time for me. My creative juices really start to flow late at night. I have gotten some of my best ideas around midnight.

Day 8

I have had a wonderful day! It is late, about 11PM. I just finished watering the potted plants. Since I have arrived, today has felt like the warmest day yet. The evening temps were so pleasant though that I decided to turn on the porch and patio lights after Cesario, my taxi driver, brought me home from the village. I watered the potted plants. I like watering plants. It is a task that allows you to think about other things while doing something that brings people happiness. Plants do make people happy whether they recognize it or not. The watering ritual definitely pleases the plants. You can almost see them wiggle with delight as the cool water bathes their parched roots. Before I sold my house, I had beautiful perennial gardens and loved getting my hands in the soil. I was surprised to discover that I may have inherited my grandmother's green thumb. Tonight even though many of the plants in Katherine's garden are different than the plants that thrive in Maine, I enjoyed that same sense of peace that caring for growing things always gives me. The heavy scent of that sexy flowering bush, Dama La Noche, filled the air, a scent beyond description, heady and intoxicating. It is the kind of dense perfume that makes my mind wander to the exotic boudoir of Scheherazade. The night sky was clear and the stars were visible. The twinkling lights of Torre Del Mar dotted the coastline. Little Corumbella and a bit farther down the mountainside the slightly larger village of Sayalonga were keeping me company with their lights, too. The cats wandered around, curiously watching me. They were hoping for a midnight snack. Oh, what the heck, I carelessly celebrated the night with them. As they nibbled away on their unexpected treats, I sipped from a small glass of wine.

The entire day was perfect. I had wandered into the village around 1:30 to join Magny, Sandra, and Ursula for lunch at Bar Marco. The little Spanish bar is a family-run business. I have eaten there often. The food is gorgeous! The prices are well below good, they are unbelievable. The girls told me that every Tuesday a lovely paella was always served. Paella is Spain's national dish. It is a rice dish full of chicken and seafood. It is enhanced by the rich gold of saffron. I was delighted with the paella. It was fresh, piping hot, and homemade. A large serving was delivered to each of us, along with bread, which I always drizzle with local olive oil. I was surprised that there was a second course that followed the paella. I ordered pork and a salad. I enjoyed this sumptuous meal plus my coffee and a large bottle of sparkling water for seven euros. I was flabbergasted! We Americans love a good deal.

It was hotter than usual today. With very full stomachs, the girls left me at the bottom of the village, beginning the steep climb to their respective homes in the village above us. On such a hot day, I was glad to be left behind. I would be joining them later on in the plaza to watch Spain play Portugal. Until then, I wound my way down to the car park, and drove home to take a nap.

Cesario arrived at precisely ocho menos quince, 7:45 PM. He is an ambitious Spanish man who runs several businesses, including a taxi service. He has a lovely family. Cesario speaks very little English, but he is patient with my Spanish, and always tries to keep a conversation going. I seemed to be his only passenger tonight, so he parked in the plaza and watched the game, too. The plaza was packed and the avid sports fans were lively and noisy, enjoying a perfect excuse to have a good time. It was a boring game, in my humble opinion, because only one goal was scored during the whole ninety minutes, but it was scored by Spain, and the excitement that engulfed the plaza was infectious.

DAY 9

Today is the last day of June! July, in Spain, is usually much hotter. My first visit to Spain was during the months of July, August and September. I rented a house in the village on Calle Triana. It was a very Spanish house with not a lot of upgrades, but my husband and I absolutely fell in love with Competa and the people. We had a lot of great neighbors on Calle Triana. They were all very friendly and kind to us. Gillian, Mo, and May Doris lived in our little circle of private houses. Pepe and his lovely wife lived next door to us. We were welcomed into that little group on equal footing with everyone. Dinner invitations were passed around. Terrace talk was engaged in regularly. Sometimes we all went out to share a meal or a drink in the evenings. It was fun! I cannot remember a time when neighborliness was so readily available.

My fourth visit to Competa has proven to be just as rewarding as all the preceding times. I have not passed an unhappy day here yet. Living outside the village is different though. Village life is convenient, full of activity, and the noise of busy lives. It offers loads of places to quickly grab your coffee or a meal if you suddenly do not feel like cooking. Walking is fun in the village, too. It is a lot of work because so much climbing is involved, but all the little narrow kissing streets, flowering potted plants, and surprise vistas from the many different levels of the village, make walking completely gratifying. I wondered how country life would compare.

Living in the campo (country) is different, but offers such a variety of benefits as to rival village life. I won't go so far as to say that I prefer one over the other, but I can say that life in the campo truly does suit me. If my husband were here, the experience would be different yet. As I have mentioned earlier, living alone in Katherine's house is a spiritual experience. I have so much opportunity to extend my living to the beautiful outdoors. The views that assault my vision every time I step outside are so incredible that I often find myself speechless with wonder. Does one ever truly get use to it? Maybe. Would I? I hope not. I have been so fortunate to live in a multitude of places around the world that offer mind-blowing land and seascapes. I always feel close to God or something bigger than myself and more powerful than all of mankind. I feel small and insignificant. Yet, at the same time, I feel so fortunate to be feasting my eyes and all of my senses on these glories. I find myself arranging my perception of life in a much more appropriate manner. Things that seemed so important often lose their status on the hierarchy of daily concerns and are replaced with natural sentiments of gratitude. These experiences heal me. They make me feel glad to be human. They make me feel humble.

Life in the campo is a little less about social opportunities and a little more about reflection. I took a midnight swim last night. The air was warm and silky. The water was pleasant and cool. The stars bright once again. I was totally relaxed. Later, I slept like a child.

Fortunately, I am not forced to live too long without companionship. When I feel like I could use a little conversation, I just hop into Katherine's orange Fiat and drive into Competa. I have already adjusted to driving in Spain. Now I rip and tear with the best of them. Look out everybody! There is an American woman behind the wheel of this car.

Last night, I had a dinner invitation to the house of Peter and Pauline. They live at the top of the village. They have a gorgeous home with a covered porch surrounded by flowering plants where we could take our meal together. Peter and Pauline are retired Brits who moved to Spain about six years ago. They rarely return to England. They are totally content with their new life in Spain. Not that they didn't love their life in England, but they are not the type of people who cannot find a home elsewhere. Spain has become their home for now.

Pauline is an amazing cook. I have to say that I actually did not know them very well. I had only been to their house once before during my last visit to Spain. Katherine invited me to tag along with her. They were hosting a party for the entire choir. I was happy to join everyone. I was surprised when they insisted on having me to dinner. I had always been curious about them. They seemed to be such happy, upbeat people. Good examples of retiring and then making the most of life after retirement.

I have always enjoyed the company of older people. Even as a young person, I was drawn to older people. In many ways, those of my own generation have been less interesting to me. As I mature, I am still largely entertained by older people who have been kind enough to share their stories, histories and wisdom with me. During my travels, the senior populations have often been the ones who have taken me under their wing. They have the time to spare. They no longer feel the need to rush off and accomplish something. Thus, we can share the hours on a park bench, in a pub, or a bar swapping stories.

We swapped great stories last night at Peter and Pauline's. They have led a very unconventional life in many ways, and they enjoy telling a good story and hearing one as well. I was entertained by their sharp wit. Also, their perspective on the village culture was interesting to hear. Pauline told me that in her opinion, there are two groups of people who fare exceptionally well in Spanish culture, children under twelve and people over sixty-five years. The Spanish are very family oriented. Their children are treated well. They deny them nothing, but also have expectations of them in regard to family commitments. Babysitters are rarely needed as everyone from aunts, uncles, and grandmas participate in the child's life. Entire families are seen in the plaza enjoying one another's company. Old people are respected and have a place of importance within the family unit. They sit on the park benches in the evenings and talk with their friends. I was impressed by Pauline's observations and had to agree that what I have seen of family life in the village supports her description. Things are changing here in Spain, as it is all over the world. When many of these wonderful, old characters pass away, it is going to alter the face of Spain immensely. They have so many memories of past times, including the Franco era and immense poverty. I have such respect and admiration for their fortitude and uncomplaining ways.

I am still reluctant to drive after dark, so I left Peter and Pauline's home around 9 PM. My return to Casa La Colina was as pleasant as usual. I enjoyed another delicious evening swim in the pool and wandered around with the cats until long after dark.

Eventually, I went inside for the night, anticipating yet another night of restful sleep.

Day 10

Today was uneventful. I deliberately chose to stick close to home. It has turned very hot, so the afternoon by the pool was the perfect solution.

I am keeping my traditional daily account sheet for Katherine while I am here. This practice is a left-over habit from my days as a principal. I used to document everything. This skill comes in handy now, too. My clients seem to appreciate receiving a record of what has transpired while they were gone. When I do longer assignments, my daily account is a great way of refreshing my own memory when needed.

Since my day was passed without outside influence from people and society, I think I will take the time this evening to write about the flamenco performance that I enjoyed with Katherine and Ian before they left. La Roca is a wonderful bar and restaurant that is owned and run by Aurelio, a very competent business man. His wife and three lovely daughters help him. This is typical of many local businesses. Many are owned and operated mostly by the family. Aurelio loves music. I have enjoyed many nights of music at La Roca.

This particular group from Malaga consisted of two dancers, two singers and two guitar players. Spanish guitar is, in my opinion, some of the best guitar music in the world. Flamenco music, in particular, is some of the most ferocious music that I have ever heard. Flamenco music continues to be honored in Spain. Perhaps pop music has a larger audience, but many young people are still committed to keeping flamenco alive. This group was outstanding. I regretted that they did not have a male dancer. The women were exquisite, but I do so love to watch the male flamenco dancers. They are like proud bullfighters. When a man and woman dance together, sparks fly! I have been fortunate to have seen some amazing artists perform since I discovered Spain.

DAY 11

I met Sandra in town this morning for coffee at El Perico. She is a new friend of mine. Early on, she had mentioned that if we could ever time it right, she might want to ask me to take care of her house. She urged me to come around and see her house, so that if we ever did have the opportunity to collaborate, I would know what her house was like beforehand. I love looking at homes and buildings. Since I was a kid, I have had a huge appreciation for the ambiance that a beautiful house offers. I like all kinds of houses, but I have a particular fondness for old homes. In Europe, old homes and buildings have been taken care of and are still very useful to the community. Sandra's house was lovely. It is in the village. Although the former owner, who was an architect, had upgraded and redesigned portions of this very large home, he was careful to maintain the old-world charm of the original building.

Spanish homes in the village are built up rather than out. In other words, there are usually three or four floors and multiple terraces at the different levels. There are usually loads of stairs to negotiate, so living in a Spanish house provides a certain measure of exercise. The terraces are substitutes for backyards, I suppose. That is where families sit to catch a breeze, eat their meals during the summer months, hang out their laundry and so forth and so on. I spoke earlier in the book about terrace life. Sandra agreed with me that there is a terrace life among neighbors that is different than the street life below. It has the charm of an Ewok village from Star Wars.

Whether Sandra and I ever manage to correlate an assignment in conjunction with a trip she takes remains to be seen, but I loved her house and would gladly live in it and care for it in the future. I have had many unexpected opportunities throughout my travels that were similar to my chance meeting with Sandra. I have not always been interested or able to avail myself of these offers. I have become acquainted with several people who own either a bed and breakfast or a small inn. One of these gorgeous properties was on the isle of Saba. The other property was in Ajijic, Mexico. Both places were utterly gorgeous. The owners wanted to know if I would consider living in these places with all expenses paid and a salary in exchange for running the establishments. I have to admit, I was interested, but in the end, because I had so carefully defined what I was looking for in a house sit, I was not tempted away from my initial dream of traveling the world. You see, although managing a bed and breakfast or an inn might be fun and even very profitable, it would have tied me to one place. I need the freedom to roam for a good while longer.

It is funny how my goals in life have changed over the course of time. There was a day when earning money, and as much as possible, consumed me. I was raising a family, putting kids through college, building a home, buying stuff that the family needed, all those things that life required in order to maintain my little piece of the American dream. I would never have guessed back then that I would have been able to walk away from the top earning years of my life or turn down a new opportunity to earn money. Yet, I have done both. I have to admit that in the beginning, I turned my back on my former life with some fear. Responsibility had been my middle name since I was a kid. It was hard for me to relinquish my perceived importance to not only my own ambitions but also my duty to others. Interestingly, after the passage of time, I began to relax in this role that I have assumed. Eventually, it dawned on me that for whatever reason, my standard of living had not perceptibly changed. I was earning a third of my former salary, but I was still living in much the same fashion that I had been living during those more lucrative times. I guess, I had always practiced the art of living within my means, and once I became totally debt free, the money I was now earning went much, much further. I no longer worry about my decision to reinvent my life according to my personal dreams. It has proven to be the right thing for me. I am much less anxious and have very little stress in my life. I enjoy the individual moments of life to a much greater extent. I am living the life that I was born to live, I think, and that is the perfect ingredient for contentment.

Incidentally, Ginger, one of the five cats that I am caring for, did not turn up for breakfast or dinner yesterday. This morning, there was still no Ginger. I sent an email to Katherine with this news, asking if Ginger had a habit of occasionally disappearing. Katherine explained that Ginger had disappeared for a few days not all that long ago. She reassured me not to worry. Ginger would more than likely reappear. If for some reason she did not, then that was something that Katherine was not prepared to worry about. I, of course, hope Ginger returns. I will keep Katherine informed.

DAY 12

Last night, it rained! It rained! I know that is not necessarily newsworthy, but you see, I have lived in Spain for an accumulated total of seven months and only on one other occasion did it rain. The first time was very late at night. It was a bold thunderstorm which was amazing. It knocked the power out in the whole of the village. The next morning the cafes got out their little gas stoves and proceeded to make coffee for everyone. It was fun wandering about the streets with the locals, everyone in good spirits. But last night's rain was different. It began to cloud up in the late afternoon and everyone was laying bets on whether there would be rain or not and what direction the clouds were headed. Rain is very unusual this time of the year. Winter is Spain's time for rain and I have never been here during that season.

So when I woke up this morning to cool, fresh breezes and soft rain, I was pleased. I had planned to go to Saturday morning market, which I have always enjoyed, but it was so pleasant just watching the clouds form and move and the rain come and go. A cool breeze wafted through the window, making the house smell fresh again. I could not decide to tear myself away. I could hear the voices in the distance of others who had decided to come to their houses in the country and enjoy the exceptional cool air. Many Spanish families have a house in the village and a house in the campo a few minutes away. Traditionally, they have enjoyed weekends and evenings at their cortinas. Today, I can hear the wailing melodies of flamenco music being played on the radio or television in a neighbor's house below me. These cool, rainy days are so utterly rare that they insist on being thoroughly enjoyed.

I was invited to join friends in the plaza at eight tonight to watch Spain play Paraguay. If the weather continues to be like this, I will not go into town. I am sure if Spain wins another game tonight and manages to stay in the world competitions that I will hear the noise made by the villagers all the way to my house in el campo.

The little village of Corumbella across the ravine has been periodically setting off dynamite for several days. My guess is that they are celebrating their patron saint or some such thing. The explosion of dynamite, as it rumbles through the ravine and bounces off the mountainsides, is a common occurrence in Spain, even late at night. It seems that someone somewhere is always celebrating something. I have grown used to it. I must admit that in some strange way it makes me feel good. I cannot explain why, something, perhaps, about the way the villages are connected through custom and tradition. The sound of the explosions are kind of like a greeting to me.

Later...........

I did not go to Competa for the game. Ursula called to confirm the reservation. I told her that I might not bother to join them tonight. I was feeling a little lazy and enjoying the cool air so much that I simply hated to go out amongst the throngs. She was as understanding as usual. Ursula seems to have a huge capacity for letting people be and do whatever pleases them. So I stayed home and to my surprise ended up watching the second half of the game on the television. This was a totally strange and unexpected action. Am I turning into a futbol fan after all?

Spain took the game against Paraguay. I rejoiced alone in the living room of Casa Colina. The windows were wide open. The evening breezes carried the sounds of band music across the ravine from Corumbella. Celebrations were happening all around me. The Spanish in their homes were cheering. Corumbella was blasting dynamite and playing music. I was tipping my glass to Spain. I was alone in the mountains, but somehow part of something communal and joyous.

On a slightly different note, Ginger came home for supper last night. He was starved. I let him into the house and fed him a larger than usual portion without the clamor of the other cats to spoil his meal. Like all cats, he offered no explanations for his recent behavior. I like that about cats. Maybe I was a cat in a previous life!

DAY 13

The rain was gone and the sun was back when I got up this morning to start my day. Tom came to clean the pool. I could have easily done that chore if Katherine and Ian had asked me to do so, but they made the arrangements before I even got here to have him come once a week to apply the chemicals and vacuum. I will probably top the pool off one more time before I leave on Thursday morning.

Yes, Thursday morning, bright and early, Katherine and Ian's son, Andrew, will pick me up and deliver me to the airport. One of the things that I always negotiate for is a ride to and from the airport. I cannot remember a time when a client was not willing to do so. Once, a taxi was arranged, on another occasion a train, but that was acceptable to me.

I have made a list of things to do before I leave on Thursday. Tina will take over the cat responsibilities and Tom will cover the pool. Tina will also water plants. She is the regular housekeeper that cleans Casa La Colina once a week or so. In so many ways, I wish that I had agreed to house sit until Katherine returned from Australia in the middle of August, but I do not make a practice of fostering regrets. I had my reasons this time for not doing the entire eight weeks. In the future, I have promised to come for the duration. Her cats will be lonely without someone around, full time. They do so appreciate the attention I give them. Whenever I step outside to do chores or just enjoy the pool or patios, they come running to join me. They like to walk around the place and help me inspect plants. When Cesario comes to pick me up in his taxi, they wait outside the gate with me until he arrives, and reluctantly see me off. When I return from an outing, they come running to greet me. They are very sweet, except for Pongo, who bit me, and remains a bit of a bully to the other cats. Even the other cats do not seem to like him very much.

I was informed last night at Ron's 4th of July party that Corumbella has been setting off dynamite because this is the week of their feria. La feria is the annual fair. All the little villages have their own village fair every year. Since these five little villages are so small, one would think that there would be a central location that would host the fair for everyone. That is not the case. Each of the villages, Canailles, Competa, Sayalonga, Archez, and Corumbella has their own fair at some point throughout the summer. The first time that I was in Competa, I experienced la feria. The people in charge of the fair came up the mountainside and set up everything in the car park at the bottom of the village where I usually park the Fiat when I go into town. For about a week, the fair provided loads of entertainment for the villagers, until the wee hours of the morning The last night involved fireworks and live entertainment. So after Cesario brought me home from celebrating the 4th of July with friends in town, I was treated to fireworks from across the ravine through the privacy of my bedroom window. It seemed like the fireworks must be a culmination of our private 4th of July celebration at Ron's house, but, of course, it was the end of la feria in Corumbella, instead.

There were six of us at Ron's for dinner. We all shared a table at the top of the house on his tiny terrace. Other families were on their terraces as well waiting for the sun to go down and the cool air to take over from the heat of the day. Greetings and inquiries were made between neighbors. It was so very lovely. I enjoyed the fine company and good conversation. I had told Cesario to meet me in the plaza around 10:30, but he reassured me when he dropped me off that I could arrive later than that if I was having a good time. He would wait in the plaza until I was finished. I joined him at 11PM.

Ron is a Mexican American. He has lived in Competa for almost twenty years. He is a handsome man. He still owns a home in Los Angeles, but rarely goes there. His real life is in Spain where he has many friends. He shares his house with two sweet dogs. He plays his cello every day. He is a kind man who I adore, a man of true style and class. I always spend time with Ron when I am in Competa. He is one of only four Americans that live here. There were two other couples present for Ron's celebration. The six of us had a marvelous time.

DAY 14

I passed the day in a most ordinary way. It was filled with daily tasks such as collecting mail, coffee in the plaza, and meeting up unexpectedly with a few friends. I was in town for about two hours and returned to do menial things like personal laundry and housework. It was a pleasant day but almost does not bear recording. It is enough to be able to say, "Today, I am content."

DAY 15

The cats located my bedroom this morning. They felt cozy enough with me to commence meowing at my window. I was in bed, dreaming with my eyes open, when I heard them. I raised myself up to look out the window. They became utterly animated. Breakfast was on their minds, of course, but I also like to think that they were missing me.

I have been sleeping heavily and for many hours this past week. I wake feeling groggy, but after a strong cup of tea, I rally nicely and begin to plan my day. When I say plan, just know that all of my plans are loosely laid. They can easily be set aside if something else comes along to tempt me.

Today, I had planned, as usual, to dress and drive into town for a cup of morning coffee. I always stop by the post office to see if there is any mail waiting for Ian and Katherine. There has been very little mail since they departed. In my opinion, no news is good news. I climbed to the middle part of the village to have my coffee. I was happily joined by Peter and Pauline. We have said our goodbyes more than once now, but each time that we do, we invariably run into each other again. We swapped more stories and meaningless chatter for a while. I finally said goodbye, again, and then crossed the plaza to the bank to use the ATM. I brought about 385 euros with me. I still had money left in my pocket, but decided to withdraw thirty euros more. While in an airport waiting, it is nice to have a little local currency in your pocket for a coffee or a bottle of water.

I decided to walk to the bottom of the village, attempting for the second time to pay a visit to my friend Lola. She is a lovely Spanish woman about my age who is a member of a rather prominent Competa family. By that I mean that her family owns property and businesses. Lola lives next door to Bar Marco where I shared the lovely paella with Magny, Ursula and Sandra about a week ago. In fact, Marco is Lola's brother. Lola has always been kind to me. I wanted to have a good chat with her, and hoped that my Spanish would hold up well enough to actually do so. I have not had a lot of practice for well over a year. If I do not use it, of course, I start to lose it. My Spanish is not fluent, but I manage. Usually, I spend loads of time with local people who speak only Spanish, whether in Competa or Mexico. My Spanish was basically learned on the streets. I lived in Guatemala with my parents for about a year when I was twelve years old. During that time, my parents turned me loose on the streets. I picked up a lot of Spanish while playing with the children of the village. I still prefer that method of learning a language, but largely because I am lazy. It is a lot of fun to practice Spanish while sharing a cup of tea or cold beer with a friend.

My Spanish saw me through a very nice conversation this morning with Lola. She and I shared stories about our children, husbands, and grandchildren. I was able to show her pictures on my iPod of Lilly. Her granddaughter, Christina, was there. She was very well behaved, allowing us to chat without interruptions. Lola's mother passed away since I last saw her. I remember her mother well. She lived to the ripe old age of ninety-three. She had been living with Lola and Antonio for some time prior to her death. Before I left, Lola talked to me about an apartment that she had recently inherited from her mother. She insisted that in the future, I need only stop and see her when I returned to Competa. She would let me live in her apartment for free, as a good friend. I was touched by the offer. I am sure Lola was sincere. She insisted over and over that the place belonged to her, and that she wanted me to live in it whenever I came to Competa. How gratifying! These are the types of friends that I have gathered around the world during my travels. Never would a tourist have such wonderful experiences. I hugged Lola goodbye with promises of returning in a year or so.

I ended up having lunch at Cafe Competa. I ate alone but enjoyed every mouthful. Afterwards, I went next door to the little market and purchased a few food items to carry home with me. By the time I had gotten home, I was hot, really hot. I drew the blinds on the side of the house facing the sun and rested with a cold drink. Then I began to accomplish things on my list of "stuff to do before I depart". I do not want to deal with last minute things tomorrow night, because I am going to join friends in the plaza for the big game between Spain and Germany. I have to admit, I am a little torn about this game. My heart is with Spain, naturally, but my daughter-in-law is from Germany and she and my son are both professors of German literature so, of course, they are hoping Germany wins. Whoever wins this game will play for the championship this coming weekend. I will not be here at that time, but I can tell you that if Spain wins the world cup, Competa will be turned upside down. I just might be able to feel the excitement all the way to America.

DAY 16

I have reached the last day of a very gratifying gig. In fact, although this job was the bare minimum time limit of what I usually require, that is no less than three weeks, I have enjoyed my time in Casa La Colina as much as any place I have ever taken care of in the past. This is true, in part, because returning to Spain is a must for me. Also, because Katherine is such a good friend, it was a very special opportunity. This glorious time in Spain has produced new opportunities for future visits to Spain. I have Sandra's house in the village and Lola's generous offer of rent-free accommodations. More than likely, there will be additional house sits for Katherine. You can see how this way of life eventually requires very little effort. I am now five plus years into living abroad. I rarely need to seek a brand-new client. I will do so again, I am sure, especially, when I am ready to see a new country. I have not been to France or Portugal, both of which remain high on my list of European countries to enjoy.

Today, however, I have Spain! I have one more glorious day with the mountains above me and the sea at my feet. Tonight, I have another evening of fun with my friends in the plaza. I have just returned from my final jaunt into Competa by car. I have to say, I have come to love those little drives along the ridge. I always stop a moment or two to drink in the first view of Competa. Although I stuck to my guns and did not go further with the car than Competa, I really enjoyed the freedom that Katherine's car afforded me. This morning, I took my coffee and breakfast in the square, collected mail, and caught up with Fernando and his little dog Sola for a chat. Fernando was the second person that my husband and I met during our first visit to Competa. Katherine was the first person we met, but Fernando helped us find the Post Office. He is a retired Spaniard who usually can be found in the plaza during the morning hours, sitting with other retired men of the village. He has a little black and white dog, Sola, who is always by his side. Fernando has remained a friend since the day that he personally walked us to the Post Office. I am told that he enquires after me throughout the year from my friend Ron.

I only spent a little time in the village this morning. I want to pack. Of course, it will not take very long to do so. I will tidy the house up a bit more, too. I also want to take a nap and a shower this afternoon before Cesario picks me up at 7 PM. When I get back from the game tonight, I will finish this entry and then go to bed. My plans are to be up by 5:30 tomorrow morning and ready to roll by 7 AM.

It is interesting that this year I did not go to the coast for even one afternoon. I think having a pool made it unnecessary. Quite frankly, I have done the coast trips many, many times before. I am no longer a sun worshipper. I actually avoid the hot sun. The mornings are cool enough to enjoy. The evenings are, too, but the afternoons require some protection from the heat. However, for those who might be here for the first time and feel compelled to do a bit of sightseeing or an occasional day trip, there are a number of places available within a very short driving distance. Torre del Mar is the first village on the coast, after winding back down the mountainside. Torre has loads of places to eat, a seaside promenade, beaches, and bars. It also has a great open market on Thursdays. Nerja is another pretty seaside resort town with about five beaches and many hotels, inns, and bed and breakfasts. Loads of foreigners live there. Malaga is a sizable city with great shopping and historical value. That is where the airport is located. There are many other seaside towns within driving distance, all offering beaches, marinas, cafes, restaurants and entertainment for tourists. Even Granada, which is in my opinion a city well worth seeing, is within a mornings drive. I have stayed there for five days once, loving every minute of it. The world famous Alhambra is in Granada. It is an amazing piece of architecture with gorgeous gardens. Flamenco performances are available, even bullfighting during the season. Spain offers a lot for the tourist.

I have been content to enjoy village life. I am almost sixty years old and have found my center. I know what brings me peace at last. Gone are the days of angst and urges. If someone had told me when I was in my thirties that life in my fifties was going to be so wonderful, I would have scoffed. Fifty seemed ancient. Youth is definitely wasted on the young. I may be approaching my sixties, but I seek and find more adventures than many people who are decades younger. It is definitely not my parent's retirement.

After the game..............

I went to bed to the sound of very high winds. My last evening in the plaza, watching the game with friends, was great! Spain is to remain in the competition until the bitter end. I will be back in the United States by this weekend when they play Holland for the big win. No matter how it turns out, it has been fun being part of the excitement that has surrounded the World Cups. Spain will play the Netherlands next and last.

Next morning....early........

I was taken aback after rising early this morning. I discovered that the harsh, unexpected winds had blown dust and plant debris all over my nicely swept patios. I found myself rushing around and sweeping up the mess before Andrew arrived. It just goes to show you that you can do your very best, but nature has a way of tossing your plans right out the door.

Andrew and I had a laugh together at my predicament as he found me a bit sweaty. In spite of the minor setback, I got everything cleaned up as best as I could, ate breakfast, fed the cats and was ready with suitcase in hand when Andrew arrived.

I am shutting down the computer after these few final words. Andrew is waiting for me. Home calls my name. Other adventures are out there. I am sure of that! They will come to me. For now, I will say my goodbyes to the cats and carry my little suitcase to the car. Heading west into the sunset, I will be back in the loving arms of my family by the end of the day. The gypsy is going home again.

Today and Tomorrow

I am currently living in my apartment, while taking care of Lilly, my granddaughter, several days a week. She will soon be a year old! She has certainly given me a very special year. Things will continue as they are until things change. That is the extent of my planning for the future these days. To enjoy the moment is everything that is real.

Adventures come to me, because I am open to all possibilities. I am sure that I will make it to India, for example. I am looking forward to exploring the French countryside. I know that I will see Scotland soon. I am certain that Spain, Mexico, and Ireland will be a part of my life for years to come. I am excited about going to China. I can imagine it all! I can already picture myself there.

I am a woman, a mother, a wife, a grandmother, a teacher, a retiree, and a good friend. I am also an international house sitter. That is what I do!

CPSIA information can be obtained at www.ICGtesting.com
Printed in the USA
LVOW061015130313

323881LV00027B/781/P